# ESSENTIALS OF
# DIVINE BREATHING

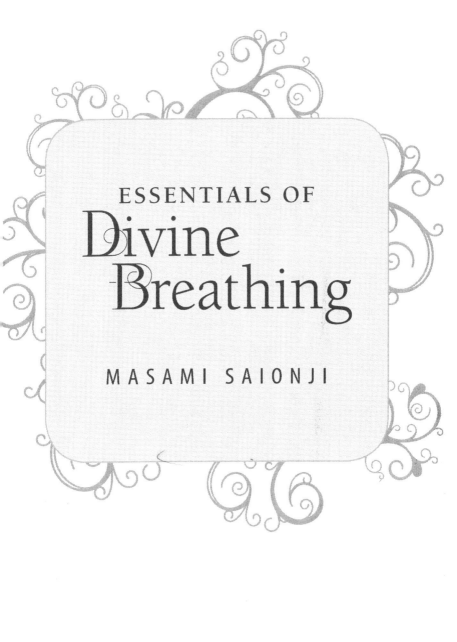

# ESSENTIALS OF
# Divine
# Breathing

## MASAMI SAIONJI

© Masami Saionji 2017

All rights reserved.

ISBN-13: 978-1-5453-6115-3

ISBN-10: 1-5453-6115-0

Senior editor and translator: Mary L. McQuaid

Contributing editors and translators: Kinuko Hamaya,
  Miyuki Ohashi, and David W. Edelstein

Cover illustration by Starline / Freepik; cover photo by
  Bedneyimages / Freepik; title page illustration by Freepik

Cover and book design by David W. Edelstein

# CONTENTS

Preface                                                              7

Chapter 1: How to Use Our Creative Energy                           11

Chapter 2: The Immense Power of the Divine                          29
Breathing Method

Chapter 3: Questions and Answers about the                          57
Divine Breathing Method

Chapter 4: Exercises in using Bright Words with                     77
Divine Breathing

Chapter 5: Creative Fields in Daily Life                           131

Appendix I: The Blue Earth is Alive                                157
  *Poem of Gratitude to Nature Delivered at the World Conservation*
  *Congress of the International Union for Conservation of Nature (IUCN),*
  *Honolulu, 2016*

Appendix II: Inspiring the World to Care                           165
  *Message to the Summit of Conscience for the Climate, Paris, 2015*

Appendix III: Introducing the Fuji Declaration                     175
  *An open letter from Masami Saionji*

Appendix IV: The Fuji Declaration                                  183

Appendix V: Further Exercises—Nationalities and                    189
Cultural Identities

Notes                                                              197

About the Author                                                   199

# Preface

*Humanity—*
*The power to make the impossible possible*
*Is bestowed on human beings alone.*
*The insight that enables you to discern, choose, and*
     *decide*
*In accordance with truth*
*Is proof that you are people of truth...*
*Holding all that is infinite,*
*Capable of manifesting anything you can imagine.*
*As soon as possible, purify your doubtful, confused*
     *hearts,*
*And awaken to eternal truth.*

(from *Cries of Life* by Masami Saionji)

Today, our world is at a critical juncture, with volatile atmospheres building up all around us. Many people are lost and confused, and have no idea how to surmount the crises that face the earth and the world of nature.

What many conscientious people do agree on is that we human beings are the ones responsible for creating these crises. This is indeed true. For many centuries and millennia, we human beings have been cutting ourselves off from great nature, and from the wellspring of perfect wisdom that resides deep within us. We have cut ourselves off from our intrinsic, sublime nature. Rather than believing in and relying on our inner source of limitless power and wisdom, we have believed in material things and relied upon others.

Now, the moment has arrived when each and every one of us must develop our own, inner abilities without depending on others. From the moment we decide to do this, our inner life power will act upon cells that have long been dormant, enabling them to work towards this goal.

To assist each person in guiding their own inner evolution and self-creation, I would like to share with you a method that emerged from the study of cosmic science[1]—a spiritual study introduced by my mentor and adoptive father, Masahisa Goi. This method is called 'divine breathing,' and it enables us to better absorb the immense power of the invisible 'cosmic essences'[2] that fill the air around us.

It is my sincere hope that in reading this book, even one more person may be inspired to believe in themselves and make the most of their one and only, precious divine life.

Masami Saionji
May 2017

# CHAPTER ONE

## HOW TO USE

# Our Creative Energy

AT THIS CRUCIAL MOMENT IN THE EARTH'S HISTORY, the world's people seem to be dividing into two streams. On the one hand, we see people who are lost and confused because they are still caught up in a materialistic mindset. Since they do not have a clear sense of the dignity and splendor of their own precious life, they feel frustrated and uneasy. Instead of living each day with feelings of peace and gratitude, they keep struggling with enemies—whether real or imagined—in the world around them. Constantly fearful of losing what they have, they try with all their might to defeat others and gain whatever advantages they can for themselves, their own families, their own groups, or their own countries.

At the same time, there are also people who care little for worldly wealth, and desire from the bottom of their hearts to contribute something to others. Their hearts are filled with respect for the earth and the environment, and they have very few feelings of anxiety over their own future. They have almost no fear of death, and think of it simply as a transition point in their sacred, never-ending life.

Every month I have the honor of joining with several thousand people like this who gather from all parts of Japan and other countries to pray together for peace on earth. Regardless of the distance, regardless of the weather, they travel in cars, buses, trains, and airplanes to a sacred spot at the foot of Mt. Fuji, where they join together in sending out waves of harmonizing energy that course through the world, purifying the violent masses of energy that are pushing the earth toward destruction.

In all countries there are people who share a similar desire to change the direction that the world is taking. These people understand that each individual on earth is responsible for the conditions that we all face today, and they know that each person's consciousness holds the power to re-create the future. Each in their own way, these people are earnestly striving to make a difference.

And yet, when I look at the lifestyles of these wonderful, peace-minded people in my own country and throughout the world, I find that, in a great many cases, when they leave their prayerful meetings and gatherings and go back to their everyday lives, the same old problems keep cropping up again. It seems like they cannot release themselves from those problems. And so, I keep asking myself, why can't they let those problems go?

We human beings are constantly stepping into the future. Whatever happened a moment ago is already part of the past. Nothing that happened in the past has the power to jump into the present moment and reappear in our lives. Yet in spite of this, many of us keep clutching at the past and drawing it back toward us. By constantly thinking about the past and reliving it in our minds, we are giving our precious life-power to it. Instead of letting the past fade away, we are re-enlivening it and forcing it to take shape again. We are doing this with the creative power of our own consciousness.

In this way, second by second, minute by minute, hour by hour and day by day, our thoughts continue to flow through force of habit. Ten years pass. Twenty years pass. Fifty years pass. And still, our minds keep grasping at the same negative situations again and again. Negative emotions, unpleasant memories, ominous expectations and beliefs—these are the kinds of situations that we are fueling and re-enlivening with the energy of our daily thought habits. I seldom see people who are able to grasp hold of bright situations and positive emotions from moment to moment in their daily lives. Ninety-nine percent of the time, even the most peace-loving people tend to reflect upon how much they have suffered, how inadequate they are, and how much they blame themselves and others. And despite all the energy they spend turning these issues over and over in their minds, they cannot find solutions. Even people who have been earnestly praying for world peace for forty or fifty years have a hard time dispelling negative thought habits and closing the door on past situations.

I am always asking people to keep their minds open and clear, to keep returning their thoughts to 'point zero.' But this is not an easy task, because our old thought habits keep on recurring automatically. The negative cycles cannot be broken until we notice them and train ourselves to change them.

## Training ourselves to think bright thoughts

One method that I often recommend is to create positive new thought habits by constantly repeating bright, encouraging words in our minds. As much as possible, I would like people to tell themselves: *I am a divine spark of life. I am the divine mind. I am always shining. My body is made up of six trillion cells, and each cell is filled with infinite love, infinite wisdom, and infinite potential. My cells are always helping and supporting each other, maintaining and recreating this marvelous, divinely-given body.*

Our bodies are such miraculous creations. Our conscious mind cannot even begin to grasp the scope of the wondrous activities that are going on in our bodies, nor can we control them through conscious effort. Our heart continues to work even while we are asleep, throughout our whole life, until the moment we die. And the same can be said about our breathing.

These wondrous functions work in accordance with the law of the universe. One shining cell catches the universal law and abides by its principles. When we know about this inexpressibly wonderful circumstance, why can't we bear it in mind? Why do we keep turning away from it?

Why is it that, when they return home from our prayer gatherings, before long even these peace-loving people find themselves again catching hold of some sort of negative incident that happened in the past, thinking: *My spouse is despicable!* or *How I loathe that person!*

Why do we keep gripping the same negative memories, the same negative feelings and emotions? It is, I think, simply because we allow ourselves to be controlled by force of habit. From moment to moment, our habit is to clutch at the same negative memories, the same unpleasant experiences, 365 days of the year. And before we know it, forty, fifty, or sixty years have passed, and there is no change in our way of thinking.

When a person is busy working, or facing a serious dilemma, they can forget those negative thoughts and apply themselves to the task at hand. But when they have some leeway in their mind, they start again. They give in to their long-standing habits. What I say is, in order to overcome those habits we have to keep inquiring into our deep, inner mind, always seeking a better and better method for aligning our thoughts with the universal divine mind, and we have to keep practicing those methods. We have to keep doing this again and again—hundreds, thousands, and millions of times.

## The sacred power of words

Since ancient times, Japanese people have believed in the sacred power of words. We believe that words are alive, and words have the power to create. We call this creative power *kotodama*. *Kotodama* literally means 'the spirit of word.' When I say kotodama, I am talking about the infinite divine power that we exert when we use divinely-inspired words. Some examples of modern-day kotodamas would be *I am a divine spark of life! I am the divine mind! Everything is absolutely getting better! Everything is perfect! Everything is transforming into waves of light! May peace prevail on Earth!*

If we repeat words like these to ourselves every day, from morning to night, without giving up, they will definitely become a habit. And as time goes on, we will find that we are less and less inclined to catch hold of negative thoughts.

*Everything is perfect! Nothing is lacking! Everything is divinely accomplished!* Kotodamas like these have the power to transform our consciousness, and they reverberate outward to our friends and family, our town, our country, the world, and all living things, creating joyful, perfect conditions in our future. When past events, past circumstances, and past memories come to mind, triggering negative emotions like regret, remorse, anger, or fear, it is okay to let them come out. In fact, they must come out. By coming out and revealing them-selves in our minds, they are able to vanish. If we suppress them, they will be unable to vanish com-pletely. So, all we need to do is to observe them as they pass through our minds and then vanish. But there is no need to struggle with them or fight against them. Instead, as they are coming out, we need to keep on repeating bright, divine-minded words at the same time—words like *This is fading away! This vibration is revealing itself in order to be purified and vanish. It's gone! It has vanished! May peace prevail on Earth! With this, everything has got-ten better! Everything is perfect! Nothing is lacking! Divinely accomplished!*

I heartily recommend repeating these kinds of kotodamas, reminding ourselves that hidden behind each and every circumstance that appears, an immense light is shining. It is the brilliant light of our innate, sacred consciousness. When we have allowed our negative thoughts, negative memories and negative expectations to vanish, this wonderful, sacred consciousness will natural-ly come shining through.

Even if they agree with this idea in principle, many people do not put it into practice. It may be because they are not willing to put forth the effort that such practice requires. Or it may be because, however hard they may try, they are overwhelmed by the force of their negative thought habits. Another possible reason is that, even though they may like the idea, they do not believe in it completely. Whatever the reason may be, I suggest that even if we don't fully grasp the effectiveness of kotodamas, we must never give up. When we are about to give up, we must take one step forward. We must continue to develop our own way of practicing them. Step by step, the effects will grow and we will become more confident.

Even if we think or say kotodamas just twenty times a day, our life will be much different from what it was before, when almost all our thoughts were turned toward the negative. Or, if we think or say a kotodama one time on a certain day, and a hundred times on the next, this, too, will make a big difference in the way our lives unfold.

Unless we do something to redirect it, our

energy naturally flows into our unconscious habits. Even if we don't feel so strongly about something, we continue to think and act in the way our habits dictate, and we ourselves may not be aware of how negative our words and actions are. This is because, when we keep feeding our energy to negative habits, they grow stronger and stronger without our even noticing it.

On the other hand, once our thought habits become positive, the same process is set in motion, and as time goes on our thoughts become brighter and brighter. At first it may take quite a bit of effort, but once a positive habit is firmly formed we can repeat it quite easily. *Nothing bad can happen to me! Everything is perfect! Everything is absolutely getting better! This problem has been resolved! It has vanished! In the real me, the original me, there is nothing negative. I am a divine life. I am one with the universal divine.* Once we catch hold of these kotodamas and make a habit of using them, they will keep surging forth, their numbers will multiply, and they will reverberate throughout humanity. Finally, the time will come when even if we try to remember what kinds of mistakes we made in the past, or what it was that made us angry, we will be unable to do so.

The bright light of our kotodamas will have permeated our consciousness, so that even during our most relaxed moments, we will spontaneously think all sorts of bright thoughts without especially trying: *I am a divine life. I am one with the divine mind. Oh, it's time to make lunch. Thank you, precious food. Thank you, divine mind. Divine-minded Japanese people. Divine-minded Syrian people. Divine-minded human beings. Divine-minded (spouse's name). Divine-minded (co-worker's name),* and so on. All negative words will have ceased to exist, and our thoughts will overflow with bright words alone.

## Developing our own spiritual method

Because people are not all the same, each individual has a different way of creating new habits. No one else can understand the experiences that we have had, and how we can each clear our own path forward. It is, of course, valuable to learn from the experiences and methods of others, but that is not enough. Ultimately, each and every one of us must develop our own spiritual method. Diversity is of the essence. If each and every human being thought and behaved in the same way, our infinite potential could not be expressed.

When we feel an affinity for a method that someone has taught us, and want to practice it, that method will serve as a precious influence for us. And once we have mastered its basic form, we naturally begin to develop our own individual expression of it. If we always simply follow and obey, never venturing to seek our own individual path, our lives cannot expand.

Meanwhile, with the state the world is in now, I feel that if humanity is to survive, more and more people need to send out as many divinely inspired words as possible. The words *May peace prevail on Earth* are, I feel, an excellent example. These words have been embraced by large numbers of people. They can be seen on peace poles, planted in hundreds of thousands of locations. They have been used at Symphony of Peace Prayers (SOPP) ceremonies held at grassroots events all over the world, and even at the United Nations.[3]

And so, as each of us continues to develop our own spiritual method, I hope that many people will incorporate the words *May peace prevail on Earth* into their own daily prayers and practices.

In the ensuing chapters, I would like to offer a special new practice to you. It is called 'divine breathing.' I hope you will find it useful.

*May peace prevail on Earth.*

# CHAPTER TWO

# The Immense Power

## OF THE DIVINE

## BREATHING METHOD

Originally published in Japanese, December 2005

A̶T THE PRESENT TIME, peace-minded people all over the world are emitting brilliantly shining, high-dimensional vibrations from their minds and bodies. These inexpressibly fine vibrations are creating bright creative fields (also called co-resonant energy fields) in various places throughout cosmic space. The high frequency of these light-filled vibrations is born from divinely-inspired words (kotodamas) such as *I am a divine spark of life. Humanity is divine. May peace prevail on Earth. Accomplished!*

These newly formed creative fields are directly linked with the universal divine mind, and are in perfect oneness with it. Because of this, they are filled with the unlimited light, peace, wisdom, and capabilities of the universal divine mind itself.

Along with these bright words, or kotodamas, peace-minded people have also been practicing what I call the divine breathing method. This is the most effective spiritual method that we have received so far. It produces remarkable new changes in us—changes that we never dreamed possible.

The first of these changes occurs when we take note of our intrinsic dignity, our own sacred nature—not with the intellect, but through our own, real-life experience. Step by step, more and more changes occur as we continue to blossom spiritually, and start to clearly recognize that all the fetters that have been binding us are nothing more than our own blind beliefs and fixed notions.

Even though we may have heard about our inner, ultimate divine nature, and are facing in that direction, for many of us it may be extremely difficult to believe in it with our whole being.

This is because the fixed ideas that we created over the course of many past existences are piled up in our subconscious mind and are always influencing us to belittle ourselves. And so, even though we have been furnished with perfect bodies that hold wondrous functions for sustaining and supporting our lives, we continue of our own accord to turn away from our precious, sacred nature.

Simply out of habit, we continue to think self-limiting thoughts. Those thoughts then generate discordant emotions that bring illness, unhappiness, and other difficulties into our lives. The negative energy of those thoughts is the source of all evils and misfortunes. Each member of humanity is stifling their divine nature in this way. We create and reinforce the scenarios of disharmony that are born from our fixed beliefs, and then we dramatize them in our daily lives.

To put it simply, our thoughts are what create and give form to things and circumstances that did not previously exist. It is important for us to be clearly aware of this. Likewise, we need to learn that when we take charge of the kinds of vibrations we send out, we can freely guide the course of our own future life.

How can we take charge of the vibrations that we send out? First and foremost, we must align ourselves with our inner, sacred truth. This is why I urge people to continually think or recite bright, powerful words (kotodamas) such as *I am a divine spark of life! Humanity is divine! Accomplished!* When we use bright phrases like these, we are perfectly at one with the divine. Just like a raindrop that merges with the great ocean, the stream of light that is our true being merges into the great divine mind. At that moment, our mind expands infinitely, and our individual past ceases to exist. Then, there is nothing that separates us from others: no differences in nationality, religion, culture, ethnicity, or skin color. All man-made boundaries vanish into nothingness.

When we release ourselves from the framework of our own, limited self-image, we regain the immense light of our original being. This is how all human beings can attain true freedom and rise above the boundaries that divide us.

## Correct breathing

In the far ancient past, when human beings first emerged on the physical plane, we were able to breathe correctly and naturally without even thinking about it. However, after we slipped into an unharmonious way of thinking, our breathing grew shallow and rough. Once we regain our true, original way of breathing and maintain it continually, our bodies will not grow decrepit with age, and our suffering and illnesses will end. This is because cosmic essences (see note 2) will be more easily received and will naturally maintain the flow of our life, healing our infirmities and ailments.

As I explained in *Genes and Cosmic Essences*, cosmic essences are inexpressibly subtle droplets that are emanations of the universal divine mind. Cosmic essences contain all the love, wisdom, and capabilities of the universal divine mind itself. They first enter the body while the baby is in the mother's womb, and after we are born we continue to receive more of them through our breathing.

This is why we practice the divine breathing method. This special breathing method helps us to regain our original, correct way of breathing, enabling us to intake an abundance of cosmic essences. In other words, through this breathing method, we attract the power of the universal divine source and make better and better use of its life-energy.

What is most important for each member of humanity is to develop our inner abilities without depending on others. When we free ourselves from our habit of depending on others, we become aware of our inner light, strength, wisdom, intuition, and power of accomplishment. This act of acknowledging our inner abilities works to activate the cells that compose our bodies. As a result, cells that have been dormant until now will start to exert their power, and work more and more vibrantly.

With the divine breathing method, we become firmly connected with the universal divine source. As we deeply inhale the cosmic essences that fill the air around us, they permeate each of our cells, expelling the fatigue, poisons, and various chemical substances that have built up there. The more each cell is freed from the toxic elements that impede it, the more cosmic life-energy can be further absorbed into the body, and the more radiantly our cells will shine. As a result, we become less and less vulnerable to illness and aging.

It is extremely difficult for toxins and fatigue, as well as the artificial and chemical substances contained in foods (artificial colorings, preservatives, and hormonal agents) to be eliminated with medications and medical treatments. And so, these substances accumulate in our body's cells and invite stubborn illnesses. The best way to expel such elements from our bodies is through profoundly deep breathing.

Here, it must be noted that the divine breathing method is entirely different from ordinary kinds of deep breathing practices. It brings in life-energy in a different way. For this reason, I suggest that, whenever they can, people meditate on their desire to be at one with the universal divine mind, and declare this intention to the great universe. In order to receive an abundance of cosmic essences directly into our bodies, it is essential that we make this kind of declaration. It enables us to concentrate better on our pure-minded desire, and to absorb as much light, power, and life-energy as possible. In this way, the vibrational energy of each of our cells is elevated, and cells that have been dormant until now are activated.

When we activate the innate power of our cells, the greater part of our ailments can be dispelled without our relying on others. There may be some conditions that require the help of doctors, medications, and surgery, but even in those cases, if we continue to practice the divine breathing method, we can bring out a remarkable healing power many times greater than we imagined possible.

Since ages past, by means of our routine thoughts and emotions, we human beings have been cutting ourselves off from great nature and from the fathomless wisdom that resides within us. From now on, however, thanks to the divine breathing method, we will be able to reconnect with that lost wisdom and awaken our immense, hidden capabilities, resolving not only our illnesses but other difficulties as well.

## Our process of evolution and self-creation

All human beings, without a single exception, have to complete their own process of evolution and self-creation. This is the life mission given to each and every one of us.

Up until now, virtually all of us have been using the power of our consciousness to create a negative self-image rather than a bright, positive one. From now on, however, this will have to change. During the 21st century, each of us must recognize our essential nature and move forward with our own light-filled evolution and self-creation. And in order to achieve this, we absolutely must free ourselves from the constraints of our long-standing blind beliefs and fixed notions. We must face up to the truth that the only things that bind us are our own fixed ideas. At the same time, we also need to acknowledge our true identity—our infinite divine nature. We must begin to think of ourselves as noble, radiantly shining beings. Once we have done this, our ailments, misfortunes, and sufferings will be greatly eased. They will continue to diminish in proportion to the degree of our own self-belief.

When our thoughts change, all the conditions that we create will start to change. When our thoughts are filled with divine awareness, our cells will be filled with light and the world we create around us will shine. No one else can do this for us. Our own thoughts—our own way of thinking, and no one else's—are the key that opens the door to our divine transformation. Apart from this, there can be no lasting solution.

At the earliest possible moment, I hope that each person will become aware that the root source of all that happens to us is found in our thinking. When we are unable to believe in our divine nature, we fall prey to fearful thinking. Our fear of illness fuels our illness, empowering it and enabling it to continue. The same can be said about failure, suffering, and misfortune. If we believe in them, if we fear them, the power of our consciousness nurtures them and pulls them toward us.

The sooner we start to believe in our inner dignity, the sooner we will be released from our suffering. Others may guide us and encourage us, but others can never change us. Only we can change ourselves.

The age of human divinity is upon us. Now is the time when we can recreate ourselves in our original divine image. The moment to do this is now. Indeed, it is for this purpose that we were born into this world.

## The prayerful nature of breathing

When our breathing stops, our divine life leaves our physical body. Breathing is the ultimate power that allows life to keep streaming through our physical being. Yet very few people are truly aware of this. Most of us go on living and breathing without giving much thought to the profound meaning that our breathing holds.

Breathing is not simply the physical process of inhaling and exhaling a gaseous substance called air. Breathing is the bond that connects our physical body with the great divine universe. It is the prayer of life that keeps this body joined with the universal divine mind.

Just like prayer, breathing keeps us connected with the universal divine. This is why I say that breathing and prayer are one and the same thing, and that all human beings are constantly praying, even though they may not be aware of it. By means of our breathing, we human beings are at all times firmly connected with heaven.

And yet, if we are breathing without an awareness of this divine connection, and without knowing that breathing is prayer, our life is not able to flow with perfect happiness and freedom. In other words, we are not fully alive. We are only half alive. This unawareness of the prayerful nature of our breathing is what keeps us from walking straight ahead along our own true path in life. Because we are not aware of our own prayer, we become confused and wander this way and that, creating side roads that lead us toward unhappiness.

From now on, as each of us gains a sense of the splendor and sanctity of our own breathing and our own prayer, one by one we will begin to live in freedom, unaffected by illness, unhappiness, worry, or distress. As our breathing merges us with the great divine mind, we experience the reality of our divine nature and can freely draw out our unlimited potential.

During the 21st century, as more and more of us start to consciously experience the wonder of our breathing, we will be able to transcend the various frameworks that we have been living in—frameworks that we created based on our standardized thinking and our cultural, sectarian, and philosophical backgrounds. This is because breathing constitutes our own complete, individual spiritual practice. When we entrust ourselves to the guidance of our breathing and our own true prayer, and breathe in the way that we are originally meant to do, we will be able to evolve and create a truly free, radiant way of living.

## Breathing is our individual spiritual practice

When we breathe properly, our bodies receive an abundance of cosmic essences, overflowing with the infiniteness of the universal divine mind. This is why I say that breathing is our own, individual spiritual practice.

*By means of divine breathing, we bring all things into being.*

*Through divine breathing, all forms of wisdom are granted to us.*

*Through divine breathing, all our dilemmas are resolved.*

*Through divine breathing, we exert the power to make the impossible possible, and all kinds of hidden abilities spring forth.*

*Through divine breathing, our mistaken ways of living are rectified.*

*Through divine breathing, our infinite healing power is manifested, peace of mind is restored, and true happiness is found.*

*Through divine breathing, each of us identifies the principles that we believe in.*

We no longer need to cling to the established tenets of the past. We no longer need to depend on them, make entreaties to them, or yield our sovereignty to them. We no longer need to enslave ourselves to them, or be abused, oppressed, or commanded by them.

Even if we are faced with all sorts of crises, even if we are visited by all sorts of difficulties and laden with problems, even if we see no chance of living to see another day, we no longer need to feel fearful. There is no need for us to flee from those conditions, circumvent them, or retreat from them. Nor is there any need for us to seek relief from another person.

We only need to wait. We only need to endure the moment. Without giving up, without becoming timid or hesitant, we only need to observe the moment that passes, holding firm until our inner life-power surges forth.

There is no need at all for us to feel rushed, or fearful, or timid. There is no need for us to expect the worst possible scenario, considering our situation to be hopeless. Rather, all we need to do is reconnect with our divine awareness, remembering that, in truth, this disagreeable circumstance is the manifestation of a distorted thought that we had in the long-forgotten past, revealing itself now at the time when it is about to fade away.

Rather than wrestling with our emotions and turning things over and over in our mind, all we need to do is hold still and submit our state of mind to the flow of nature. All we need to do is to steadily practice the divine breathing method.

Also, I think it is important for us to clearly and firmly tell ourselves that the various worries that are germinating in our minds do not yet have any fixed consequences. Everything is still in a formative process. We freely determine whatever consequences we choose. We determine them by believing in them.

Here, I would like to caution everyone not to be swept up in any longtime habit they might have of negative thinking. This habit is the blind spot that we human beings created when we fell into ignorance and fear. We must become aware of this blind spot, and remove ourselves from it. If we allow ourselves to be controlled by negative thinking, we are easily driven toward negative outcomes. Because we are overly fearful about conditions that might appear in the future, we pour our creative energy into those worrisome conditions, which actually causes them to take shape. And so, even though we do not wish to be drawn into those circumstances, we are unable to turn things in a better direction.

I think it can be helpful for us to keep reminding ourselves that the seeds of all the worries and pains that are looming in our hearts are not yet linked to any fixed outcomes, and that the 'you' and the 'I' who exist here and now are the ones who determine what will appear in our future. It is not that God brings about shining results by acting upon us from the outside, nor does any particular saint, or other person. Rather, it is the God-given creative power that we hold within us that makes it happen.

Up to now, a great many people have deeply believed that good outcomes would be given to them if they clung to God and depended on God. However, now that we have entered the 21st century, more and more people are beginning to notice that the divine mind does not simply rescue us from the outside. Rather, the divine mind is at work within us. People are starting to sense that the aim of our life is to evolve and create ourselves, and to give real expression to our hidden potential by exerting our own free will.

The person who creates and brings about good outcomes is our own divine self—no one else. Humanity has reached the stage where we can learn this principle and experience it. When our consciousness has evolved to where we can catch hold of this principle, each of us can generate good outcomes by continually polishing and uplifting ourselves from moment to moment. And the method that enables us to do this with remarkable effectiveness is the divine breathing method—the breathing method of life and prayer. By practicing this method, we become conscious of the ultimate principle that is inscribed in each of our genes: that all forms of life are firmly joined with the will of the universal divine.

By means of our quiet, spiritualized breathing, we clearly recognize that the ominous conditions we have been dreading have not yet manifested on the phenomenal plane.[4] On the other hand, people who have not yet observed this truth often exert their free will in a detrimental way. During the formative stages, when those negative outcomes have not yet been established, people are overwhelmed by their fears and jump to the conclusion that those unwanted outcomes are definitely going to appear. Then, by persuading themselves of this and believing it, they create the conditions for those adverse phenomena to take shape.

Instead of doing this, it is essential that we draw forth the conditions for success, healing, happiness, and life by means of the breathing and the prayer that connect us directly with the universal divine mind during the formative stages—before those outcomes have manifested. We need to draw forth those positive conditions with the power of our belief. We need to guide ourselves toward good, radiant outcomes by making full use of the free will and creativity given equally to each of us, and to manifest them in the phenomenal world.

Through the divine breathing method, we inquire into our ultimate divine truth, come face to face with it, and give expression to it from moment to moment in our daily words and actions. This takes repeated efforts, but these efforts are indispensable for creating our own noble and precious way of living. For as long as we live in this world, these kinds of worthy efforts—aimed at drawing out our ultimate truth—are the key to everything.

## What kinds of efforts do we need?

Over the course of time, our efforts gradually diverged further from truth, and degenerated into mean, unwholesome efforts stained with bribery and flattery, as people connived to entrap others, deceive them, and kick them down. Yet no matter how many ambitions and desires we might satisfy with such efforts, the results cannot last for long. Sooner or later, the returns of all our sullied efforts are sure to come back and appear in front of us.

Now that we have reached the 21st century, the only way we can truly move forward is for each of us to make sincere, honest, well-meaning efforts, and let them accumulate one by one. There may be times when it feels like we are assailed by fiercely raging storms, there may be times when we feel timid and fainthearted, and there may be times when we fall into pessimism and self-doubt. At such times, it is important to gather up our strength and take one step forward.

As we continue to recreate our lives with the divine breathing method, step by step we will feel our inner life-energy flowing forth within us.

Sometimes we may be aware of bright, intuitive flashes recurring in our minds, and we may start to notice that our thinking is changing. As our ideas and emotions come more and more under our control, it occurs to us that negative thinking is not in accord with our way of breathing.

In this way, unharmonious thoughts are purified and vanish from our mind. In time, our sensitivities become so enhanced that we are able to discern bright vibrations reverberating outward from the interior of our being. At that time, we will be conscious of the vast, inner potential that has been closed off until now.

Once we have reached this point, we know that we have made it! Now, a steady stream of bright thoughts is constantly surging from our mind, and all we need to do is to go on creating positive outcomes with our unwavering self-belief.

Light-filled words (kotodamas) are power itself. They are the power that transforms our unruly emotions and creates for us—and for humanity—a future brimming with peace, radiance, and stability.

## Absorbing cosmic essences

The divine breathing method was conveyed to us through cosmic science (see note 1), and it enables us to absorb the harmonizing power of cosmic essences to transmute unhappy future conditions into happy ones before they emerge in the tangible world. With the divine breathing method, we can redirect the course of our precious lives.

We cannot begin to imagine the immense power that lies dormant in each of our cells. When human beings concentrate on manifesting the infinite abilities that we each hold within us, aided by the incredible workings of cosmic essences, all pain and anguish will vanish from this world.

Everything depends on our own decisions and efforts. We need to clearly observe how our thoughts and emotions are creating our personalities from moment to moment. When we do, this awareness becomes an opportunity for us to polish and uplift ourselves without limit.

I think each of us needs to set a goal for the kind of life we wish to lead, and steadily guide ourselves in that direction. There is no need to waver and no need to rush. We only need to take it step by step.

As long as we do not halt our efforts, there is no limit to what we can accomplish. It is our own heart's desire and our own free will that turn possibilities into realities.

The essential thing is never to give up on our inner potential. We must not turn away from it. We must respect it, cherish it, and believe in it. Even if we have had bitter experiences in the past, we must continue to encourage ourselves, telling ourselves that thanks to those bitter experiences, everything is sure to get better. We must believe that a positive outcome that has not yet revealed itself even once is going to appear today. This is the kind of belief that we need to nurture. This is the kind of effort that we need to put forth.

What happens when people do not exert control over their own thoughts or follow the directives of their own true mind? Inevitably, they end up depending on others and allowing others to control them. This can never make anyone truly happy, because when we place ourselves under other people's control, it means that we are denying the worth of our own existence. We may not be doing this consciously, and we may not want to admit it, but it is indeed so. Without wholly believing in our sacred, divine nature, we keep repeating this way of life, carried along by the inertia of our own bad habits.

For better or for worse, all of us human beings are living as we have determined to live. Nothing will change for us until we start making changes in ourselves.

The task that each of us faces is to rise above our present self. We need to step up to a higher perspective. And to do this, it is essential that we understand our inner, sacred nature and allow it to express itself. We have to make that the basis of our life.

In the natural order of things, the 'me' of today ought to be better than the 'me' of yesterday. We are the ones who make this happen for ourselves. Whatever the time, whatever the place, whatever the situation, we each need to make large-scale efforts and call forth tremendous power in order to rise above our present self. If we make good use of the divine breathing method, we can definitely call forth this power.

What a terrible waste it is to place limits on our own abilities, then confine ourselves within the frameworks of those limitations. We human beings ought not to confer power on the word and the notion of 'limitation.' We ought to firmly know that what we decide is what we create.

Giving up is a decision. Relinquishing is also a decision. Each moment within the flow of our endless life contains an infinite array of possibilities. From this moment forward, I hope that we will make the most of them. I hope that we will each take great care of our precious divine life.

Each one of us, without a single exception, is the planner and the creator of our own future. At this point in history, peace-minded people need to pave the way for others by recognizing this truth and by creating our own shining way of living. Those who understand this, and make daily efforts to put it into practice, are given a special role to play in bringing happiness to the world, and are greatly blessed by the universe.

Let us keep thinking: *Everything is perfect, nothing is lacking, everything is fulfilled and divinely accomplished!*

# CHAPTER THREE

# Questions
## *and* Answers
## ABOUT THE DIVINE
## BREATHING METHOD

In the following interview, Masami Saionji's editorial staff ask her
some questions about how to practice the divine breathing method.
The interview was held on February 9, 2016, and the article
was first published in May 2016.

*For more than ten years now you have been guiding us in practicing the divine breathing method. Could you please give us an explanation of what this practice entails?*

Certainly. To explain it briefly, breathing is the bond that connects us with the great divine universe. However, many people's breathing has become shallow and irregular. When we breathe slowly and deeply, it becomes easier for us to live vibrantly and take in the cosmic essences that are overflowing in universal space.

As I mentioned earlier, cosmic essences are emanations of the universal divine mind itself, and they contain all the love, wisdom, and capabilities of the universe. Divine breathing is a special breathing method that enables us to receive large numbers of cosmic essences, and retain them in the body for as long as possible.

I will explain the divine breathing method in further detail, but at this point I will just give you a quick overview of the entire practice.

Before you start practicing the divine breathing method I suggest that you relax your mind, sit or stand up straight, firm up your lower torso, and slowly and naturally inhale and exhale a few times through the nose. Next, silently make a personal declaration to the universal divine mind, expressing your intent to become one with it. Then, using the method that I am about to describe, inhale while silently reciting a word or a phrase that calls to your inner divine nature. Pause slightly before exhaling. Then exhale while silently reciting a word or a phrase that calls to the divine nature of all humanity.

You can choose whatever words or phrases you like. Be sure to use words or phrases that resonate well with you and give you a good feeling.

Here are a couple of examples:

## Example 1

Inhale thinking: *divine mind* (one or more times)
(Pause slightly before exhaling)
Exhale thinking: *May peace prevail on Earth* (one or more times)

## Example 2

Inhale thinking: *divine-minded (your own name)* (one or more
    times)
(Pause slightly before exhaling)
Exhale thinking: *divine-minded human beings* (one or more times)

The choice of words or phrases is up to you. It is important to use wordings that you like, and that are meaningful to you. And it is important that the words be filled with love, respect, and gratitude toward yourself, all people, and all living things.

As you continue to practice this method, you may wish to change the words. This is fine. It is important to keep observing how a recitation makes you feel, and to change the words when you wish to. This is a part of your process of evolution and self-creation.

When we use uplifting recitations along with the divine breathing method, we are able to naturally connect with our inner, sacred nature. The divine breathing method can also be practiced on its own, without the recitations, but practicing the recitations enables us to better focus on our inner divine mind, and this, in turn, helps us to further refine and enhance our breathing.

In practicing this method, I think we need to set our sights on the long-term effects. It is important to keep practicing it again and again. Of course, we can expect to feel some positive effects right from the beginning, but when we have practiced it many, many times, the method really becomes our own.

*Some of us find that the divine breathing method takes a lot of concentration and is not so easy to master.*

Yes, mastering this method takes quite a bit of practice. But if we take it one step at a time, we can experience wonderful changes in our thoughts and in our bodies. At the same time, divine breathing unleashes a tremendous power that permeates all of humanity with a great divine light. This is what Goi Sensei[5] calls 'the simultaneous awakening of the individual and humanity.'

What I suggest is that, even if you may not be able to do the breathing correctly at the beginning, you try to get a complete picture of how the divine breathing method is meant to be practiced, and form an image of it in your mind. Then, as you continue to practice day by day, your body and your breathing will naturally approach closer and closer to the correct image that you are holding in your mind.

*Could you please describe that image to us?*

Yes. First, imagine that as you are slowly inhaling through the nose, your lungs are naturally expanding and filling with bright currents of cosmic essences, overflowing with the power of harmony. As we inhale, we focus our attention on the *tanden*—the area slightly below the navel—and we rapidly tighten our abdomen as if we are pulling the navel back, closer and closer to the spine. As our chest keeps expanding, we continue to pull back the navel more and more. Then, before exhaling, we briefly hold our breath.

Throughout the practice—while inhaling, while holding our breath, and while exhaling— we keep our abdomen firm, and we imagine that our navel and our back are very close together, as if touching each other. Also, as we exhale, we try not to exhale in one big gust, but little by little, in a thin but steady stream of air.

How are we able to exhale little by little? By drawing the navel even further back—even closer to the spine. By imagining this extremely narrow space between our navel and the spine, we are able to exhale a thinner stream of air.

*Why is it important to exhale with a thin stream of air?*

If we exhale in one great burst, a lot of cosmic essences rush out of the body all at once. But by exhaling in a thin stream, we enable more cosmic essences to remain in the body for a longer time. As a result, the cosmic essences in the body can continue to work powerfully. They circulate very rapidly, making the body feel warm. The body feels warm because the cosmic essences in our body are ignited. This is the key to the divine breathing method. But at first, it is enough to simply hold this kind of image in your mind.

After we finish exhaling, our consciousness is still focused on keeping the navel and the spine pulled close together, and with that image in mind we start again to inhale a thin stream of air while pulling the navel back even further.

When we keep the navel and the spine almost touching each other as we inhale, it has the effect of pulling in a very thin stream of air. So, the air that we inhale (through the nose) will not be the kind of air that we ordinarily receive. Because we are inhaling through a very narrow space, unnecessary elements are kept out, and only the purest air, overflowing with cosmic essences, is able to enter the body.

As we continue to do this again and again, the cosmic essences contained within our body are ignited more and more. After we have continued practicing this method for three, four, or five years, it will come to us much more easily, and the effects will be absolutely marvelous!

So, at the beginning, keep this image in your mind, and keep practicing it day by day without giving up. Because you are holding the correct image in your mind, that image will permeate your efforts, and step by step you will naturally guide yourself toward perfect, correct breathing.

*Is there a special meaning behind focusing on the navel as we are breathing?*

Yes. The navel plays a very important role in the body. When a baby is growing in the mother's womb, the umbilical cord is connected to the mother's navel, and cosmic essences flow into the baby's body through this connection. And as the baby grows up to be an adult, it remains connected with the universal source of life, and cosmic essences continue to enter the body.

When we practice the divine breathing method, thanks to the *tanden* we can naturally experience oneness with and gratitude toward the universal source of our life. On the other hand, when we inhale without using this method, a few cosmic essences might come in, but not in such concentrated form. A great many cosmic essences are attracted to us when we practice the divine breathing method. They rush in, as if drawn by a magnet.

*Is there anything else we need to pay attention to as we practice the divine breathing method?*

Yes. To keep the cosmic essences circulating powerfully in our body, we also need to tighten our bottom. Our body has many openings, such as the eyes, the nose, the ears, the mouth, and pores, and cosmic essences can exit the body through those openings. By tightening our bottom, and at the same time keeping the *tanden* firm (the *tanden* is an area in the lower abdomen, slightly below the navel), we enable the cosmic essences to continue circulating throughout the body, diminishing the toxic elements in our cells and the stagnation in our blood flow, letting our natural healing power surge forth. Then, our brain functions will also become more active. This is why in the original martial arts and other spiritual disciplines, students are cautioned to constantly keep tightening their bottom.

In daily life, if we keep inhaling and exhaling in a careless manner, this area can become too relaxed, and cosmic essences can easily exit the body. As a result, we can easily lose energy. So, we must take care to keep it tightly closed. For the divine breathing method to work properly, a lot of cosmic essences have to build up in the body. The work of cosmic essences keeps us in good health and helps us to maintain good bodily control.

At the same time, if we maintain a feeling of gratitude toward the cosmic essences, and toward everything in nature, it naturally becomes easier for us to maintain proper breathing. Our thoughts and emotions always affect our breathing, and our breathing affects our thoughts and emotions.

Good habits like these are developed over time, and it takes steady efforts to make it happen. As we keep practicing, we learn how beneficial the divine breathing method is. Each in our own way, we learn how to keep improving our practice and make the most of it.

In any spiritual or artistic discipline, be it

flower arrangement, martial arts, painting pictures, or whatever it may be, we are taught an established form that we keep practicing again and again. This form contains the basics of the discipline that we are learning. In Japanese, this form is called *kata*. We practice this form again and again until we can do it perfectly. Then, with this form as our foundation, we each develop our own unique creativity and power of action. This is the kind of effort that is needed by all of us. It is the effort we make to master the basic form. The divine breathing method that I am teaching is a kind of basic form that people can master.

*With the divine breathing method we were taught that while inhaling we can make a sound, and we can focus on a point in the back of the head, imagining that the air fills the body until it reaches the area behind the eyes…*

Yes. As we are inhaling we focus our attention on an area in the back of the head, behind the eyes, and we also make a slight sound that we associate with this spot. This sound is like the sound of the universe, and it helps us to concentrate better on our breathing. After a while we can do the breathing without this sound, but at the beginning it can be helpful to make the sound.

It is from this spot at the back of the head that we can see the universe. This spot is called our 'divine eye.' With our physical eyes we can see the surfaces of things, but when our divine eye opens up, the universe comes into view. When the cosmic essences in our bodies are activated through the divine breathing method, all our spiritual and divine functions—inspiration, intuition, divine vision, and so on—are developed. This method is so important—I cannot overemphasize how important it is.

*Is there anything else we need to know about using recitations with the divine breathing method?*

Yes. In the examples I gave at the start, I mentioned that between the inhale and the exhale, we briefly hold our breath. This can be just a very slight pause. However, as you continue to practice, you may find that you are able to hold your breath for a longer time. While you are holding your breath, you can make a short affirmation. One very powerful affirmation is the word *Accomplished!* Thinking *Accomplished!* is like affirming that we have connected with the divine universe. For several years, peace-minded people have been making this affirmation, and it holds a tremendous power. When we hold our breath, the creative power of our thoughts is intensified, because the cosmic essences in our *tanden* are tightly concentrated together and poised for action.

There is another, longer affirmation that I also recommend. It is to think: *Everything is perfect! Nothing is lacking! Divinely accomplished!* This affirmation enables us to focus even more powerfully on our latent, infinite potential. When we make this affirmation, it reminds everything in the universe of its innate, divine perfection.

So, if you would like to use this longer affirmation, the practice would go something like this:

Inhale thinking: *divine-minded (your own name)* (one or more times)

Hold your breath thinking: *Everything is perfect! Nothing is lacking! Divinely accomplished!*

Exhale thinking: *divine-minded human beings* (one or more times)

*Thank you. Please go on with what you were saying about correct practice of the divine breathing method.*

Correct practice of the divine breathing method is not something that can be conferred on us from the outside. We have to practice it over and over again, for a lengthy period of time. Only then can it be really ours.

The same is true for the method of *Fading Away—May peace prevail on Earth*, something else that we learned from Masahisa Goi. We can read about this method and understand the principle behind it, but unless we practice it over and over again, consciously and sincerely, it will not come alive for us. Whatever the method may be, under-standing the principle is an important first step, but we have to keep on practicing it.

In any practice we undertake, if we simply

listen to what others say, and do nothing about it ourselves, we remain dependent on others. We are not developing our own divine awareness. It is by practicing something again and again that we begin to notice things. We begin to discern what is going on, and we know what we should do. Many things become clear to us. At the same time, we connect more and more firmly with our own spiritual protectors who are always guiding and safeguarding us from within.

And so, I would like to encourage everyone to continue practicing the divine breathing method, and to keep holding an image of it in your mind. It really feels good! Step by step, you will get better at it, and you will become able to breathe more slowly and more smoothly than before. To increase the length of your breath by even two seconds, it takes a lot of genuine practice and effort. So, let's continue making this effort without giving up!

Now that some 10,000 people have been practicing this method for several years, it should be easier for others to do the same. The tide is in motion. When I say 'tide,' I mean that an energy field—a field of creative energy—has been established. The first time we practiced the divine breathing method, it was quite a challenge, but now, when new people try it, it is easier for them to do, because the creative field for it is expanding.

This is how the circles of peace are spreading out. One by one, as each human being continues to think peacefully and breathe peacefully, our own, individual creative field for peace grows bigger and stronger. At the same time, it merges with the creative fields of others, and the large-scale creative field for peace works more powerfully. This is how we each empower ourselves and exert a positive influence on the world.

*On behalf of our readers, thank you for this valuable interview!*

The pleasure is mine. *May peace prevail on Earth.*

# CHAPTER FOUR

# Exercises

## *in using*

# Bright Words

## WITH THE DIVINE

## BREATHING METHOD

WITH THE STATE THE WORLD IS IN NOW, I think it has become clear that if we just sit idly by and wait for governments to create peace—thinking that it is their responsibility and not ours—peace will never come about. Rather, the world will surely go to ruin.

Many people seem to think that an individual's own thoughts and words are without impact, and that if we are to contribute to world harmony we have to take some sort of visible action that can be observed in the tangible world. However, I feel that nothing could be further from the truth. It is our invisible actions—our thoughts and our words—that create fields of energy that later man-ifest in various forms, situations, and events.

The ability to use words is innate to all hu-man beings, and all of us are capable of exerting the creative power that words hold. At the same time, each person has their own habits and way of thinking, and if we are to make the best use of words, we must each develop our own way of doing it. In this chapter I would like to introduce some exercises that contain bright, shining words. These exercises have emerged from the experienc-es of individual people, and I hope that they may serve as a useful reference for you.

You can try these exercises while meditating, while walking, jogging, swimming, sewing, pre-paring meals, and so on. And of course you can use them while practicing the divine breathing method. Also, if you have started creating 'living mandalas' (refer to my book and website *The Earth Healer's Handbook*), you might wish to write some of the same words in your handwritten mandalas.

Try these exercises to see how they work for you. You can also create new exercises of your own. The possibilities are infinite!

## EXERCISE 1

# Making silent shouts in your mind

*Bright, shining words have a tremendous power to purify and uplift our state of mind, and they can inspire us and change the course of our future. At the same time, they touch other people, animals, plants, rocks, rivers, and the ground we walk on by means of their vibrations. If you find yourself feeling weak or depressed, try making silent shouts in your mind using light-filled, encouraging words like the ones shown below. You can say them aloud when you are alone, or you can say them in your mind when other people are around.*

*The words in this exercise are shown in sets of seven, but you can say them as many times as you like. Even one time is fine.*

*Each of these exercises helps to uplift the individual, humanity, and all life on earth, all at the same time.*

Divine mind!

Divine mind!

Divine mind!

Divine mind!

Divine mind!

Divine mind!

Divine mind!

~~~~~~~~~~~~~~~~~~~~~~~~~~~~~~~~~~~~~~~~~~~~

World Peace!

World Peace!

World Peace!

World Peace!

World Peace!

World Peace!

World Peace!

~~~~~~~~~~~~~~~~~~~~~~~~~~~~~~~~~~~~~~~~~~~~

Divine life!
Divine life!
Divine life!
Divine life!
Divine life!
Divine life!
Divine life!

~~~~~~~~~~~~~~~~~~~~~~~~~~~~~~~~~~~~~~~

Thank you God!

Thank you God!

Thank you God!

Thank you God!

Thank you God!

Thank you God!

Thank you God!

~~~~~~~~~~~~~~~~~~~~~~~~~~~~~~~~~~~~~~~

Divine-minded (your own name)!
Divine-minded (your own name)!
Divine-minded (your own name)!
Divine-minded (your own name)!
Divine-minded (your own name)!
Divine-minded (your own name)!
Divine-minded (your own name)!

Divine-minded (someone else's name)!

Divine-minded (someone else's name)!

Divine-minded (someone else's name)!

Divine-minded (someone else's name)!

Divine-minded (someone else's name)!

Divine-minded (someone else's name)!

Divine-minded (someone else's name)!

Divine-minded (Israeli) people!
Divine-minded (Israeli) people!
Divine-minded (Israeli) people!
Divine-minded (Israeli) people!
Divine-minded (Israeli) people!
Divine-minded (Israeli) people!
Divine-minded (Israeli) people!

*Note: This exercise can be used for any nationality or cultural group if you change the word in parentheses to a different word. See Appendix V.*

Divine-minded (Palestinian) people!
Divine-minded (Palestinian) people!
Divine-minded (Palestinian) people!
Divine-minded (Palestinian) people!
Divine-minded (Palestinian) people!
Divine-minded (Palestinian) people!
Divine-minded (Palestinian) people!

*Note: This exercise can be used for any nationality or cultural group if you change the word in parentheses to a different word. See Appendix V.*

Divine-minded (North Korean) people!
Divine-minded (North Korean) people!
Divine-minded (North Korean) people!
Divine-minded (North Korean) people!
Divine-minded (North Korean) people!
Divine-minded (North Korean) people!
Divine-minded (North Korean) people!

*Note: This exercise can be used for any nationality or cultural group if you change the word in parentheses to a different word. See Appendix V.*

Divine-minded (Chinese) President!
Divine-minded (Chinese) President!
Divine-minded (Chinese) President!
Divine-minded (Chinese) President!
Divine-minded (Chinese) President!
Divine-minded (Chinese) President!
Divine-minded (Chinese) President!

*Note: This exercise can be used for any leadership position in the world if you change the word in parentheses and use the matching title, such as 'Prime Minister' and so on.*

Infinite love!

Infinite love!

Infinite love!

Infinite love!

Infinite love!

Infinite love!

Infinite love!

Infinite harmony!
Infinite harmony!
Infinite harmony!
Infinite harmony!
Infinite harmony!
Infinite harmony!
Infinite harmony!

Infinite conciliation!
Infinite conciliation!
Infinite conciliation!
Infinite conciliation!
Infinite conciliation!
Infinite conciliation!
Infinite conciliation!

Infinite forgiveness!
Infinite forgiveness!
Infinite forgiveness!
Infinite forgiveness!
Infinite forgiveness!
Infinite forgiveness!
Infinite forgiveness!

~~~~~~~~~~~~~~~~~~~~~~~~~~~~~~~~~~

Infinite gratitude!
Infinite gratitude!
Infinite gratitude!
Infinite gratitude!
Infinite gratitude!
Infinite gratitude!
Infinite gratitude!

~~~~~~~~~~~~~~~~~~~~~~~~~~~~~~~~~~

Thank you, dear earth!
Thank you, dear earth!
Thank you, dear earth!
Thank you, dear earth!
Thank you, dear earth!
Thank you, dear earth!
Thank you, dear earth!

Thank you, dear ocean!
Thank you, dear ocean!
Thank you, dear ocean!
Thank you, dear ocean!
Thank you, dear ocean!
Thank you, dear ocean!
Thank you, dear ocean!

Thank you, dear mountains!

Thank you, dear mountains!

Thank you, dear mountains!

Thank you, dear mountains!

Thank you, dear mountains!

Thank you, dear mountains!

Thank you, dear mountains!

Thank you, dear animals!

Thank you, dear animals!

Thank you, dear animals!

Thank you, dear animals!

Thank you, dear animals!

Thank you, dear animals!

Thank you, dear animals!

~~~~~~~~~~~~~~~~~~~~~~~~~~~~~~~~~~~~~~~~~~

Thank you, dear plants!

Thank you, dear plants!

Thank you, dear plants!

Thank you, dear plants!

Thank you, dear plants!

Thank you, dear plants!

Thank you, dear plants!

~~~~~~~~~~~~~~~~~~~~~~~~~~~~~~~~~~~~~~~~~~

Thank you, dear minerals!
Thank you, dear minerals!
Thank you, dear minerals!
Thank you, dear minerals!
Thank you, dear minerals!
Thank you, dear minerals!
Thank you, dear minerals!

Thank you, precious water!
Thank you, precious water!
Thank you, precious water!
Thank you, precious water!
Thank you, precious water!
Thank you, precious water!
Thank you, precious water!

~~~~~~~~~~~~~~~~~~~~~~~~~~~~~~~~~~~~

Thank you, precious food!
Thank you, precious food!
Thank you, precious food!
Thank you, precious food!
Thank you, precious food!
Thank you, precious food!
Thank you, precious food!

~~~~~~~~~~~~~~~~~~~~~~~~~~~~~~~~~~~~

Thank you, dear air!
Thank you, dear air!
Thank you, dear air!
Thank you, dear air!
Thank you, dear air!
Thank you, dear air!
Thank you, dear air!

Thank you, dear lungs!

Thank you, dear lungs!

Thank you, dear lungs!

Thank you, dear lungs!

Thank you, dear lungs!

Thank you, dear lungs!

Thank you, dear lungs!

Thank you, dear muscles!
Thank you, dear muscles!
Thank you, dear muscles!
Thank you, dear muscles!
Thank you, dear muscles!
Thank you, dear muscles!
Thank you, dear muscles!

Thank you, dear cells!
Thank you, dear cells!
Thank you, dear cells!
Thank you, dear cells!
Thank you, dear cells!
Thank you, dear cells!
Thank you, dear cells!

Thank you, healthy heart!

Thank you, healthy heart!

Thank you, healthy heart!

Thank you, healthy heart!

Thank you, healthy heart!

Thank you, healthy heart!

Thank you, healthy heart!

## EXERCISE 2

# *Making silent shouts while holding your breath*

*Try making silent shouts while holding your breath. The words are shown in sets of seven, but you can say them as many times as you like.*

*This practice is especially helpful when we are experiencing unwelcome circumstances, unpleasant thoughts, or worries over the future, because when we hold our breath it becomes easier to concentrate on the words. This, in turn, increases the power of the words.*

*Each of these exercises helps to uplift the individual, humanity, and all life on earth, all at the same time.*

*Inhale thinking:*

It's fading away *(one or more times)*

*Hold your breath thinking:*

Fading away! Fading away! Fading away!
Fading away! Fading away! Fading away!
Fading away!

*Exhale thinking:*

May peace prevail on Earth *(one or more times)*

Note: This exercise means that unwelcome conditions are fading
away, so that brighter conditions can appear.

~~~~~~~~~~~~~~~~~~~~~~~~~~~~~~~~~~~~~~~~~~~~~~~

*Inhale thinking:*

It's vanished! *(one or more times)*

*Hold your breath thinking:*

Vanished! Vanished! Vanished! Vanished!
Vanished! Vanished! Vanished!

*Exhale thinking:*

May peace prevail on Earth *(one or more times)*

*Note: This exercise means that unwelcome conditions have
vanished, and brighter conditions can appear.*

~~~~~~~~~~~~~~~~~~~~~~~~~~~~~~~~~~~~~~~~~~~~~~~

*Inhale thinking:*

Everything is absolutely getting better!
*(one or more times)*

*Hold your breath thinking:*

Absolutely! Absolutely! Absolutely!
Absolutely! Absolutely! Absolutely!
Absolutely!

*Exhale thinking:*

May peace prevail on Earth *(one or more times)*

*Inhale thinking:*

Everything is absolutely getting better!
*(one or more times)*

*Hold your breath thinking:*

Getting better! Getting better! Getting better! Getting better! Getting better! Getting better! Getting better!

*Exhale thinking:*

May peace prevail on Earth *(one or more times)*

*Inhale thinking:*

May peace prevail on Earth! *(one or more times)*

*Hold your breath thinking:*

Accomplished! Accomplished! Accomplished! Accomplished! Accomplished! Accomplished! Accomplished!

*Exhale thinking:*

May peace prevail on Earth *(one or more times)*

*Inhale thinking:*

Everything is perfect! *(one or more times)*

*Hold your breath thinking:*

Perfect! Perfect! Perfect! Perfect!
Perfect! Perfect! Perfect!

*Exhale thinking:*

May peace prevail on Earth *(one or more times)*

*Inhale thinking:*

Divine-minded (your own name)!
*(one or more times)*

*Hold your breath thinking:*

Divine-minded (someone else's name)!

Divine-minded (someone else's name)!

Divine-minded (someone else's name)!

Divine-minded (someone else's name)!

Divine-minded (someone else's name)!

Divine-minded (someone else's name)!

Divine-minded (someone else's name)!

*Exhale thinking:*

Divine-minded human beings!
*(one or more times)*

**Note:** *Perhaps you have noticed that large-scale phrases, such as* May peace prevail on Earth, *or* Divine-minded human beings, *have a very uplifting effect. When you create your own exercises, I recommend that you add some large-scale phrases as often as you can.*

*Also, when you use a bright word or phrase, try it out many times to see how it makes you feel. If the words seem too long, or if they don't make you feel happy even after repeating them again and again, you may wish to change them to something that feels right. When you are practicing on your own, you don't need to follow what other people are doing. You can freely choose the words and phrases that work for you, create new ones, and arrange them in the way you like.*

# *Reciting poems, prayers, or verses in your mind*

*There may be times when it makes you feel happy to recite your favorite poems, prayers, or verses in your mind.*

*The first five examples in this exercise are taken from my book* The Earth Healer's Handbook. *The next two examples are about people. In the examples about people, we can mention qualities that the person has, and also qualities that we would like to further bring out in that person.*

*You can use this practice anytime—while walking, relaxing, and so on.*

## *Gratitude to the Earth*

We thank the love of the universe
for supporting our lives through the earth.
Beloved earth
giver of life
home to all life
how can we thank you?
May peace prevail on Earth.
On behalf of humanity
we offer our gratitude
to the earth.

~~~~~~~~~~~~~~~~~~~~~~~~~~~~~~~~~~~~~~~~~~

## *Gratitude to the Ocean*

We thank the love of the universe

for sustaining our lives with the ocean.

Deep ocean

vast ocean

abundant ocean

how can we thank you?

May peace prevail on Earth.

On behalf of humanity

we offer our gratitude

to the ocean.

~~~~~~~~~~~~~~~~~~~~~~~~~~~~~~~~~~~~~~~~~~

### Gratitude to Mountains

We thank the love of the universe
for blessing our lives with mountains.
Noble mountains,
mystical mountains, purified mountains
how can we thank you?
May peace prevail on Earth.
On behalf of humanity
we offer our gratitude
to all mountains.

## *Gratitude to Water*

On behalf of humanity
We thank the love of the universe
for enlivening us with water.
Pure water, clear water, dancing water
how can we thank you?
May peace prevail on Earth.
On behalf of humanity
we offer our gratitude
to all water.

### Gratitude to Animals
We thank the love of the universe
for blessing our lives with animals.
Innocent animals, affectionate animals
helpful animals
how can we thank you?
May peace prevail on Earth.
On behalf of humanity
we offer our gratitude
to all animals.

~~~~~~~~~~~~~~~~~~~~~~~~~~~~~~~~~~~~~~~~~~~~~~~

## *Gratitude to Plants*

On behalf of humanity
We thank the love of the universe
for gracing our lives with plants.
Beautiful plants, joyful plants, life-giving plants
how can we thank you?
May peace prevail on Earth.
On behalf of humanity
we offer our gratitude
to all plants.

~~~~~~~~~~~~~~~~~~~~~~~~~~~~~~~~~~~~~~~~~~~~~~~

~~~~~~~~~~~~~~~~~~~~~

*Gratitude to (someone's name) (1)*
On behalf of humanity
We thank the love of the universe
for the shining existence of (name).
Big-hearted (name), joyful (name)
how can we thank you?
May peace prevail on Earth.
On behalf of humanity
we offer our gratitude
To peace-loving (name).

~~~~~~~~~~~~~~~~~~~~~

## Gratitude to (someone's name) (2)

Divine-minded (name)

Divine-minded (name)

Divine-minded (name)

Divine-minded (name)

Divine-minded (name)

Divine-minded (name)

Divine-minded (name)

how can we thank you?

May peace prevail on Earth.

On behalf of humanity

we thank the love of the universe

for the prayerful existence

of divine-minded (name).

# CHAPTER FIVE

# Creative
# Fields

## IN DAILY LIFE

Originally published in Japanese, August 2008

DURING THE 20TH CENTURY, science and religion (or spirituality) were treated as if they were totally separate fields. Each of them was considered a world unto itself, having nothing at all to do with the other. Nowadays, however, this trend seems to be changing. We see some spiritual leaders who interest themselves in the findings of science, and we also see scientists who recognize the existence of the spirit or soul.

And so it happens that, as a person involved in personal and spiritual development, I am sometimes called upon by scientists to describe my own spiritual experiences. Surprisingly, however,

I find that this is by no means easy to do. I think this is because such experiences are an integral part of my normal daily life. While living in this physical realm and interacting with people from day to day, I am at all times clearly aware of the spirituality of each one of them. I naturally hear the voices of plants, animals, and other living things, and I feel their joys and sorrows as if they were my own.

What further complicates the task is that I seldom think about or remember what I have experienced in the past. This is because my consciousness is always rooted in the present moment. My primary focus in life is to make the most of the 'now.' However, since I have been asked to do so, I will try to give a description of some of the things I perceive and experience in my usual daily life.

When I look at the people around me, I see the same attributes in them that are visible to anyone else: their physical form, the clothes they are wearing, their posture, their gestures, and their facial expressions. At the same time, I also see the fields of creative energy that they are generating.

The thoughts, words, and emotions that we

human beings emit from moment to moment are constantly streaming forth from our bodies, forming creative fields which are visible in various colors, forms, and shapes. Some of these creative fields are hazy and cloudy in appearance, and they hover around the person in indeterminate patterns. Others are extremely tenacious, and they twine tightly around the person like a resilient string. Emotions like happiness and affection appear in shining colors, and they envelop the person in a halo-like radiance. Emotions like worry, fear, and animosity reflect smoky colors, and they adhere closely to the person in a suffocating manner.

Each thought or emotion holds its own unique form of creative energy, and thoughts having a similar frequency band together to form a homogeneous creative field around the person who emitted them. When the amassed energy of a particular creative field has accumulated to a critical point, and is triggered by some external circumstance, it is released in some form on the visible plane. This manifestation might occur in the form of an event, happening, or situation that emerges in the person's life. It might take shape in the form of an encounter with another person. Or, it might manifest itself in words that one hears, or reads, or that pop up unexpectedly in one's own mind. Once this manifestation has occurred, the energy held within the creative field is depleted to just that extent.

## Kinds of creative fields

From what I have observed, there are as many kinds of creative fields as there are human thoughts and emotions. On the positive side, there are creative fields for qualities such as thoughtfulness, optimism, gentleness, dignity, purity, cleanliness, goodness, and sincerity. There are creative fields for feelings like happiness, enthusiasm, friendship, courage, admiration, gratitude, trust, respect for life, respect for nature, and humanitarian love. There are creative fields for behavior such as praise, encouragement, acceptance, generosity, and forgiveness. There are creative fields for phenomena like inspiration, healing, fulfillment, improvement, and accomplishment. And there are creative fields for conditions such as peace, harmony, truth, sanctity, abundance, and bliss.

On the negative side, there are creative fields for feelings like pessimism, frustration, anxiety, self-blame, self-pity, self-doubt, self-hate, self-justification, guilt, and a thirst for revenge. There are creative fields for phenomena such as discrimination, suicide, accidents, wars, and disasters. There are also creative fields for fixed ideas, such as a belief in sin, a belief in punishment, a belief in defeat, a belief in failure, and a belief in illness and poverty.

## How do creative fields get started?

Because creative fields like those mentioned above shape our personalities, our health, our relationships, and the conditions around us, I would like to talk a bit about how these fields get started.

The energy of any thought or word, whatever it might be, holds the potential for generating a creative field. However, unless several thoughts or words of the same type are emitted, a creative field will not be formed. Just one thought, in and of itself, will quickly lose impetus unless it is reinforced by the energy of other thoughts that resemble it.

If numerous thoughts or words of the same type are emitted, their energy will band together and the rudiments of a creative field will take shape. Once this rudimentary creative field has been formed, as new energy is added to it, its mass increases and it consolidates into a cohesive creative field. As this creative field continues to grow, it exerts a stronger and stronger influence on the person's will, decisions, and behavior.

## Collective creative fields

The activity of a creative field becomes further invigorated when similar creative fields are generated by other people. This is because creative fields having the same vibrational frequency tend to merge together, forming large-scale collective creative fields. These collective creative fields can be extremely pervasive. The bigger they are, the more powerfully they respond to thoughts emitting from people in various places.

Let us say, for example, that someone idly thinks of committing suicide. To begin with, his wish to commit suicide is not particularly strong. Unfortunately, however, his idle thoughts attract the vibrations of a big collective creative field for committing suicide. These vibrations exert considerable influence on his thinking and behavior. Unless positive influences intervene, or unless the person himself consciously rejects those negative vibrations, he might end up actually committing suicide.

When it comes to positive thoughts, the scenario becomes much brighter. Let us say that for a long time, someone has been in the habit of blaming and underestimating herself. Even over trivial things, she finds fault with herself and reflects upon self-demeaning words such as: *I am selfish, my soul is tarnished, I am unworthy, I am unappreciated, I am unloved.* Each time such words pass through her mind, they summon the arrival of a matching kind of energy from a large-scale collective creative field for self-blame. The influx of this energy plunges her into a state of intense unhappiness. As a result, she finds it quite difficult to stay in a good mood from day to day.

Fortunately, however, she comes in touch with a book about the importance of using bright words. Or perhaps she has joined a useful workshop or attended an SOPP ceremony.[6] All of a sudden, she realizes what a disservice she has been doing to herself with her self-demeaning way of thinking. With firm determination, she makes up her mind to create a new way of living based on positive words. She likes the term 'peace-minded,' so she starts with that. She creates a kind of litany around the words, combining them with her own name. Let's say her name is Susan. Susan's recitation goes like this:

*Peace-minded Susan*
*Peace-minded Susan*
*Peace-minded Susan*
*Peace-minded Susan*
*Peace-minded Susan*
*Peace-minded Susan*
*Peace-minded Susan*
*How can we thank you?*

*May peace prevail on Earth.*
*On behalf of humanity*
*We thank the love of the universe*
*For the dignified existence*
*of peace-minded Susan.*

Again and again, she repeats these words to herself in a continuous rhythm—like a poem or a melody. When unpleasant emotions arise, she deeply inhales, holds her breath, and starts to repeat the words in her mind. Sometimes she changes the words a little, based on the inspiration of the moment. To uplift her thoughts regarding other people, she also tries creating similar litanies using those people's names.

Because respecting our own existence—and the existence of others—is in tune with the harmony of the universe, these positive words attract a flow of shining, positive energy from all over the universe. And because she adds the humanitarian message *May peace prevail on Earth*, as well as words of gratitude, Susan is able to access an incredibly uplifting power overflowing with love. Not only does this bring happiness to her, it also contributes to a vast creative field for happiness on the planet Earth and throughout the universe.

## Taking positive control of our creative process

Much has been written and said about the creative power of thoughts and words—especially words. But it seems to me that few people truly understand this power. If they understood it, how could they go on using words so carelessly? Like children playing with fire, human beings are spewing out negative words without considering what the effects might be. Here and now, I would like to clearly state that the energy of our every word, once it has been spoken, flies into the creative fields that are forming around us, intensifying their activity. Not only do these creative fields give shape to our own individual circumstances, they also give rise to world conditions of poverty or abundance, respect or discrimination, destruction or rebirth, war or peace.

How can we take positive control of our own individual creative processes? How can we dissolve the unharmonious fields that we have unknowingly created? Our first step, I feel, should be to steadily observe our own thoughts and words to gain a sense of what kinds of fields we are now creating. Next, I suggest that we train ourselves to cancel out all negative words as soon as they come to mind by countering them with bright ones. At the same time, I recommend that we make up our minds to free ourselves from all our destructive beliefs and transform them into constructive ones.

To do this, we must clearly know that, whatever we think and believe, our energy flows in that direction. If we believe in our potential for building a peaceful, happy world, and envision beautiful, joy-filled circumstances in our mind, our thought-energy jumps ahead of us and forms a creative field for those kinds of situations. As that field fills with energy, its power increases. Eventually, it becomes so strong that it can pull us toward the peaceful future that we have envisioned. When we have reached that stage, it is no longer necessary for us to make vigorous efforts. We are so closely connected with the field for world peace that we can merge into it without effort.

It is, indeed, effective for us to envision small-scale goals, and many of us may be doing this naturally. I feel, however, that we also need to hold a large-scale vision in our minds and consciously pour our energy into it. This is why I urge everyone to make a habit of embracing a large-scale goal such as world peace.

## Deactivating destructive fields

A growing number of people are doing this by means of light-filled recitations. As in the example of Susan, mentioned above, each of us can use the words of our choice. Likewise, our choice of words can change as our way of thinking changes. A recitation can be a prayer, a poem, a belief, or a goal. The important thing is to choose words that are good for us, for all people, and for all life on earth.

How do we practice a light-filled recitation? Let us say that you have chosen the words *Everything is perfect! Nothing is Lacking! Accomplished!*

Whenever you have a chance, repeat these words silently in your mind (or say them aloud if you are not bothering anyone). You could also try incorporating them with your breathing, using exercises like the ones in chapter 4.[7]

Many people have found that, through this practice, their thought-habits really do change, and their circumstances do get better. And although we may not notice it, our recitations are definitely spreading out and having an influence on other people, the earth, and the universe.

Here, I would like to encourage everyone to keep repeating words of gratitude to nature. Many people find that by chiseling such words into their consciousness, they naturally begin to feel more grateful toward the earth and the environment. As the creative fields for gratitude to nature keep growing, the spirit of gratitude will enfold the earth, nature will be revived, and all living things will be able to live together in harmony.

When I see people practicing gratitude to nature, or praying intently for peace on earth, I see a clear white light emanating from their bodies. This light envelops the destructive fields that project wars, environmental disasters, and other tragedies, purifying them and reducing their intensity.

## An 'other-worldly' experience

Here I would like to tell you about my earliest memory of an 'other-worldly' experience. When I was 19 years old, I suddenly became ill during a family trip to Okinawa. I fell unconscious at a site where, at the end of World War II, many young Okinawan girls had committed suicide. I was rushed to the hospital and later taken back to Tokyo.

My illness was diagnosed as a cerebral tumor, and the option of surgery seemed unpromising. For the next year, I had seizures every day and was unable to keep food down. I became very thin and gradually lost my eyesight, then my hearing.

Starting from the early days of my illness, I was visited every day by Goi Sensei, whom I had met when I was about fifteen, before I started volunteering in his world peace prayer movement.

After I became ill, Goi Sensei would pray with me each day.

Goi Sensei had often told me about my spiritual protectors (he called them 'guardian divinities and guardian spirits'). However, until then, I had always refused to listen because I disliked topics relating to anything psychic or spiritual. While I was ill, however, my feelings changed and I got into the habit of praying to my guardian divinity.

During my illness, I used to see grotesque visions of human beings without faces, or with missing eyes, noses, or other bodily features. But thanks to Goi Sensei's encouragement, I never gave in to fear or tried to run away from these phantom beings. I steadily continued to pray for world peace, and spoke to them reassuringly, saying things like: *You are all right! God loves you. God is taking care of you. You will be fine! Give thanks to God. Think of peace. Think 'May peace prevail on Earth.'*

In time, these visions gradually diminished and ceased. Eventually my hearing returned, as did my eyesight. But for a long time, I was weak and continued to have seizures. Feeling that my existence must surely be a burden on my family, I often thought about dying.

## When I looked at the sun

Whenever I felt fearful or uneasy, I would pray for world peace. One day, while I was praying intently, I happened to glance up at the window above my bed. It was about midday. Since my eyesight was getting better, I was able to see the shining sun. I remember thinking: *Oh, the sun is shining! How lovely and warm it is. It melts the cold and warms my body. Thank you, dear sun! Thank you!*

As I was thinking this, the sun began to approach me. It kept getting bigger and bigger. I felt as though it was falling straight down from the sky. The sun came closer and closer and, when it was right in front of me, it merged into my body.

Just then, I saw the light of my guardian divinity. It was a warm, loving light—not a human form—and I knew at once that this was my guardian divinity. She spoke to me, not with words, but with an instantaneous flash of meaning lasting for less than a second. Put into words, this is what she said: *I am always with you, just as you see me now. I am your guardian divinity. Everyone has a guardian divinity, shining directly behind them at all times, guiding and protecting them. I know how much you have been suffering, but you must stay in this world. You have work to do here. Your job is to tell others that guardian divinities and guardian spirits really do exist. Now that you have seen me with your own eyes, you know that it is true, so you can surely tell them. If you don't do anything else from now on it is all right. Just tell people about their guardian divinities and guardian spirits.*

When I received this flash of meaning from my guardian divinity, I felt gently enfolded in her love. I felt totally comfortable and at peace. It was then that I noticed that I was no longer in my physical body. I was looking down at my body from above. I could see the energy flowing out from my fingers and toes. *Oh*, I thought, *the energy is leaving my body. How interesting! This must be what death is!*

Then, recalling what my guardian divinity had said, I was instantly back in my body.

## A marvelous influx of universal divine energy

It was after this near-death experience that I gained a deep sense of the infiniteness of the universe. I became clearly aware that there is indeed a wellspring of life—an expanse of unlimited potential—existing at the source of the universe. From one moment to the next, each of us is sustained by the life-energy that is continually flowing to us from the universal source.

At a given time, the wellspring of the universe radiated various fields of life—mineral life, plant life, animal life, human life, and so on. Human life was imbued with a creative capacity—the ability to generate creative fields. Whether we intend to or not, we are constantly creating. For human beings, to exist means to create.

Creative fields that are bright and positive naturally connect with the universal divine mind. So, no matter how many destructive fields might exist in this world, we must never feel discouraged. When we use our energy for positive aims—aims that are good for the earth and for all living things—we will be supported and enlivened by a marvelous influx of universal divine energy. At that time, the creative fields for world peace will surely expand and grow. This process has started already.

## My experience of meditation

When I go into meditation, I simply concentrate on oneness with the essential vibration of the universe. My breathing becomes deeper, slower, and more spiritualized. I can feel my cells expanding through the surrounding space until there is no dividing line between myself and space, nor between myself and others. My consciousness still recognizes that I am Masami Saionji, but there is no boundary to my existence. I am one with the universe, one with the Earth, one with all living things, existing beyond time and space.

Because we are all connected, we can understand each other's mind and feelings. We can understand what has happened in the past and how to guide the future. When we have experienced this oneness, there is no further need for us to strive, or endure, or make efforts—no need to learn from any teacher. We only need to be in oneness. We only need to make the connection.

Until we make this connection, we need to keep turning our thoughts to the wellspring of life, the source of infinite potential. We must not give up. Even if the goal seems far away, we must take one step forward. We must try, try, and try.

We must always keep in mind that, in truth, there are no dividing lines between people. When we know that dividing lines do not exist, we understand that when we speak, think, or move, the effects instantly spread to others. This knowledge brings with it a sense of responsibility. We understand that we must exert a positive influence on others.

And so, we need to brighten our consciousness, bringing it closer and closer to the universal divine source. That brightness will instantly touch others, sparking them to evolve and to create themselves further.

If we want to avoid giving our energy to unharmonious creative fields, we need to closely observe and take positive control of our words, thoughts, and actions. In this way, unharmonious fields will eventually disintegrate and vanish, and only bright ones will remain.

*May peace prevail on Earth.*

# Appendices

# A Poem of Gratitude to Nature

*The following poem was first delivered by Masami Saionji in September 2016, at the World Conservation Congress held by the International Union for Conservation of Nature (IUCN) in Honolulu, Hawaii, USA.*

*Headquartered in Switzerland, the IUCN is the world's largest and most diverse environmental network, with 1,300 member organizations and staff in more than 50 countries. Every four years the IUCN World Conservation Congress meets to set priorities and agree on the Union's work program.*

*The theme of the 2016 Congress was "Planet at the Crossroads," emphasizing the need to take action now in order to ensure the survival of humanity and life on earth.*

*Masami Saionji and her husband Hiroo were invited to take part in the Conservation and Spirituality 'Journey,' to share their wisdom and experience with Congress participants and to speak about the Fuji*

*Declaration (see Appendices III and IV). The Conservation and Spirituality Journey hosted numerous 'Knowledge Cafés,' where small groups gathered to discuss various topics in an intimate setting.*

*The Saionjis took part in two Knowledge Cafés, titled "Experiences on Conservation and Spirituality" and "Spirituality and Conservation: from Inspiration to Action." They brought with them a large handwritten mandala[8] with expressions of gratitude to water, which was displayed in one of the conference rooms at the Convention Center, and was also used as a centerpiece for the first Knowledge Café, with participants sitting around it.*

*At the "Experiences on Conservation and Spirituality" Café, Mrs. Saionji began by leading everyone in a breathing exercise before giving her talk, which ended with a recitation from her original poem, presented on the following pages.*

## The Blue Earth Is Alive

by Masami Saionji

The blue earth is alive.
The mystical earth is awakening.
Mountains, rivers, and oceans—
All of nature is full of life,
Dancing with beating hearts.
Within them the mind of God is alive.

Even stones, rocks, and minerals
Are slowly and deeply breathing
Even if we cannot see it with our eyes.
I clearly find God
Shining in such places.

Animals, plants, and fishes, even small insects are active,
Overflowing with the joyful vibrations of God.

The sky is clear and pure
And the sun shines all around.
The land is at ease.

Our bodies and all our cells are shining,
All beings are living together in harmony,
Emitting the light of life.

This is how the planet Earth is meant to be.
But what is the reality on Earth today?

How long has it been since all peoples and nations
Cried out to protect our environment?

Through humanity's self-serving greed,
The Earth has been severely damaged,
The continuation of the species has been endangered,
And we have pursued a path to ruin.
We human beings, each and every one of us, have broken our
    agreement with nature.
We are destroying ecosystems
And bringing harm to one precious life after another.
Now, each of us, all of us, must admit to our wrongdoing.
Fellow human beings, is this the way it should be?
Is this the way we should leave it?

Now, each and every one of us must stand up,
Equally bearing the Earth's heavy burden
And fulfilling our responsibility.

No further can any of us continue our assault on the Earth.
From here on, we walk a path not of destruction, but of creation.
No longer has any of us the right to plunder that which sustains
    life,
That which the Earth has infinitely and freely supplied.

Fellow human beings, the time has come to wake up.
For those newly born, our posterity,
We can no longer snatch away the resources needed for life.
The time has come
To ask the sick and damaged Earth to forgive us
And to repay its favors.
Fellow human beings,
As soon as possible, let us ask the Earth for forgiveness,
Unite our hearts one and all,
And, with infinite gratitude, offer ourselves to the Earth.

The time is now.
If we let it pass, no solution is in sight.

Now is the time for all human beings to awaken to the
tremendous blessings freely given by our planet.

On behalf of all humanity, let us offer gratitude to the Earth.

Gratitude to the Earth is the wholehearted awareness of each
and every one of us.
Healing the Earth is the sincere atonement of each and every one
of us.
Harmonizing the Earth is the deep love of each and every one
of us.
Bringing peace to the Earth is the heartfelt joy of each and every
one of us.
Shining on the Earth is the genuine awakening of each and every
one of us.

Dear planet Earth, please accept our penitence,
Forgive our arrogance and self-serving behavior.
At long last, all humanity will be ashamed of our ignorance
And shift to a higher dimensional consciousness.

The planet Earth is one living, evolving entity.
No longer will any human being hinder its evolution.
No longer will any human being destroy its harmony.

Today, earthly humanity is returning to its true self.
We are awakening to our innate sacred consciousness.
We hear the footsteps of a spiritual civilization,
And here today, a new path is dawning.

The Earth, newly revived,
Moves forward along with humanity on a path of evolution and
     self-creation.
The glory of planet Earth is here!
Infinite Gratitude to the Earth!

# Message to the Summit of Conscience for the Climate

## Paris, 2015

*In 2015 Masami Saionji was invited by François Hollande, the President of France, to take part in a special world summit called The Summit of Conscience for the Climate, held in Paris on July 21. The theme of the summit was "Why do I care?" and its purpose was to gather Nobel Prize Laureates and other conscientious leaders to discuss ways of safeguarding the planet, preliminary to the United Nations Climate Change talks (Paris COP 2015) held in December.*

*Due to unforeseen circumstances Ms. Saionji was unable to attend in person, and her husband, Hiroo Saionji, participated on her behalf.*

*The following is Masami Saionji's message to the summit.*

## Inspiring the World to Care

*Inspiring the world to care, and igniting the will to act for the climate.* When I first saw these words, describing the theme of the Third Plenary, I was filled with a deep sense of awe and admiration.

When I reflect upon the daily lives of the Earth's people, it seems to me that inspiring ourselves to care is the most important, most precious thing we can do. Indeed, I feel that inspiring ourselves to care may be our primary purpose in living. After all, what could be more worthwhile than making moment-to-moment efforts to bring out the best in ourselves and in the people around us, so that we may contribute something positive to the health and happiness of the planet?

When we strive to inspire ourselves and inspire others, I think we can be greatly encouraged by observing the lives of people we admire and respect. For me, one such person is my husband's great-grandfather, Kinmochi Saionji, a dedicated pacifist who served twice as Prime Minister of Japan. He served his country under three emperors—Meiji, Taisho, and Showa—and his guiding wish was to preserve the peace-loving nature of the Japanese people. Before the outbreak of World War II he made strenuous efforts to prevent Japan from entering the war.

Kinmochi Saionji was a student of French, and while in his twenties he spent several years in France and other parts of Europe. He became a close friend of Georges Clémenceau, who later served as Prime Minister of France. Like Clémenceau, he was firmly opposed to all forms of racial discrimination. Until his death he dedicated his life to inspiring the world to care, and when he passed away at the age of 91 he was honored at a state funeral. Even today he is well remembered for his last, dying words: *There is no need at all for Japan to become a military power. Rather, Japan must go down in history as an honorable nation, a nation that everyone can respect.*

What I admire most about Kinmochi Saionji is his steadfast belief in the dignity of life. More than anything else, I feel that the world's people need to revive and develop this sense of dignity and respect for all living things.

## What kind of beings are we?

What is it that inhibits the blossoming of this inborn sense of dignity? The answer, I think, is borders—borders that separate one nation from another, one religion from another, one ethnic group from another. Although it is vital for us to respect and encourage diversity, I think it is also essential for us to sense that we all share in the one, all-encompassing life of the universe. If we continue to identify ourselves in terms of the borders that divide us, always thinking, *I am Japanese! I am French! I am Greek! I am a Catholic! I am an atheist! I am a democrat!* or *I am a member of this group or that party!* peace and harmony will never take root in our society.

What is the one thought that continues to wreak havoc in each person's mind? It is the thought of conflict and discrimination. We are always running a race against someone. We are always competing with someone. We are always seeing ourselves in terms of oppositions: the winners versus the losers, the rich versus the poor, the hungry versus the well fed. For as long as we see ourselves only as members of a particular group or nation, there will always be some who are prideful and arrogant, and others who feel inferior and resentful.

To put an end to this way of living, I feel that we need to change our perspective. We need to start seeing ourselves as citizens of Earth and the universe. We need to calm our emotions and return to a deeper awareness. We need to recognize each individual as a sublime, noble spirit—a "divine spark of the universe." I can clearly state from my own experience that this is absolutely true. It is just that we have forgotten it. We fell into a path of ignorance when we deserted our spiritual nature and began devoting ourselves to materialism.

## Abandoning our belief in scarcity

In our deeper, more spiritual nature, we are filled with an expansive sense of beauty and richness. Our minds overflow with a bright, healthy feeling. Our spiritual self is totally unlike the materialistic one. The materialistic mind is what created the notion of scarcity. A lack of goods, a lack of money, a lack of food, a lack of land, a lack of respect, a lack of education, a lack of love: the materialistic mind believes only in what is finite, and sees everything as being in short supply. This fixed idea—this notion that something is lacking—produces painful effects on the world of nature. It creates a lack of water, a lack of clean air, a lack of natural resources, a lack of vegetation. It then focuses its attention on what is lacking, and tries to seize more of it.

How can we put an end to this vicious cycle? How can we change direction?

Before we can resolve issues like climate change and environmental destruction, I feel that each of us must return to our innate, expansive self and abandon our belief in scarcity. We must return to the immense world of our untapped talents. When we do, a new world will open up for us. Once we can think of ourselves as unlimited beings, all our anxieties will be transcended. Our greed will be transcended. The borders that divide us will be transcended.

What good does it do to continue chasing

after finite resources? Even if wealthy people continue to acquire more and more property and more and more money, until the end of their lives they will never feel satisfied. This is because their inner, noble spirit is being stifled. This noble spirit, this divine spark of the universe, is the voice that keeps saying to us, *I want to contribute something! I want to be of service to others! I want to live with gratitude! I want to feel at one with the land, the trees, the mountains, and the oceans!* This inner voice is the source of our life power and the guide to our happiness.

When we take a narrow, self-serving perspective, we can never find true solutions. It is like trying to treat an ailment simply by relieving its symptoms. In the same way, if we try to relieve the effects of climate change only for the benefit of our own nation, it can bring no lasting improvement.

It is time to inspire ourselves to care deeply about Great Nature. Testing atomic weapons, digging into the earth in search of fossil fuels, conducting dangerous tests in the ocean—this kind of selfish behavior kills innocent insects, animals, plants, and microorganisms. How can we think that nature will continue to tolerate such behavior?

## Fostering a sustainable world civilization

In many traditional cultures, like that of the Ainu people of northern Japan, human beings naturally feel grateful for the blessings of nature. From generation to generation, they developed sustainable cultures based on give-and-take, affectionate relationships with nature. The prayerful thoughts of human beings, the feelings of admiration and gratitude they send out, turn into light-filled vibrations that flow into the animals, the air, the mountains and seas. I cannot help but feel that if modern-day people had imitated this way of life, we would never have done such harm to our environment.

But let us take heart. It is not too late to make a new start. Simply by listening to our inner sacred voice, we can inspire ourselves to take a step forward.

We human beings seldom transform ourselves overnight. But if even one person takes a step forward it will surely influence others. Starting with just one step, let us make up our minds to inspire ourselves to care, and inspire the world to take action.

*May peace prevail on Earth.*

# Introducing the Fuji Declaration

## an open letter from Masami Saionji

*The following open letter was issued by Masami Saionji prior to the launching of the Fuji Declaration in May 2015. The Fuji Declaration was co-initiated by Dr. Ervin Laszlo (Founder and President, The Club of Budapest), Mr. Hiroo Saionji (President, The Goi Peace Foundation), and Ms. Masami Saionji (Chairperson, The Goi Peace Foundation). For further information, kindly visit **fujideclaration.org**.*

From moment to moment, the world is relentlessly changing. No one can stop changes from taking place. The question is, in what direction are these changes taking us? Are they opening doorways to a wondrous future, or are they driving us toward ruin and devastation?

During the 20th century, this world experienced a rapid development in material culture and civilization. However, due to the dominance of materialistic values, and the priority given to economic expansion, humanity has been following an extremely dangerous path.

Until now, almost everyone has been striving to lay their hands on limited material resources—resources that are in short supply. Rather than drawing out the infinite resources within us, most of us have set our sights on materialistic aims—physical comforts that will make our life more agreeable. Money, land, houses, cars, delicious things to eat; position, fame, control over others—for a great many people, aims like these are seen as the ultimate reason for living.

Because our thinking is rooted in a belief in limitation, we have created a way of life where everything is lacking: a lack of food, a lack of money, a lack of health, a lack of friendship, a lack of love. Now, all over the world, we can see the results of this way of living. We can see widespread poverty, illness, greed, catastrophes, and environmental destruction. And with each passing day, these conditions are growing more and more severe.

Why is there so much suffering? Why is there so much discrimination, so much mistrust and discontent? All this, I believe, results from our belief in limitation. In struggling with each other to gain limited benefits, we adopted the rule of 'survival of the fittest' and let ourselves be controlled by it. Divisions arose between the winners and the losers, the weak and the strong, the rich and the poor. Those who could grasp the largest share of goods could enjoy a life of ease, while others were left empty-handed. And even when we attained more material benefits than we could ever use, we lived in constant fear of losing them.

Our abuse of great nature has brought us to where the earth is in danger of losing its existence.

What are we to do? At this late date, how can we change direction?

Some people feel that we can change the world by tackling each problem and remedying the tangible conditions one by one. Yet unless we make a fundamental change in the mindset that gave rise to them, the same conditions will surely emerge again.

How, then, can we change our underlying attitudes? How can we re-enliven our own hearts? Our only choice, I feel, is to return to our starting point and begin again. We have to search deeply within us to find what is lasting and real.

First, I feel, we need to stop and reflect on what it is that each human heart holds dear. We often hear people call for their rights, demanding freedom and equality. Yet of what value are freedom and equality unless we use them well? We must wake up and see that, sooner or later, we will have to take responsibility for the results of all our decisions—all that we have said and done.

To live responsibly, first and foremost, each of us needs to know the dignity of our own precious life. This, I feel, is our starting point. And when we can sense the dignity of our own life, inevitably, we will hold a feeling of awe toward the lives of others. Today, most of us have forgotten this feeling of awe, respect, and love. Most are still dominated by fear and selfishness. For most, the guiding thought is *As long as I am all right, nothing else matters.*

The hostility, discrimination, chaos and greed that overrun this world all come from the same source—a loss of reverence for the lives of others. Here and now, each human being needs to make a new start and begin caring about the future of humanity. Each human being needs to take just one step forward. It need not be a big step—just something we are capable of. From the moment we take that first step, our lives will start to change. Step by step, doubt will be supplanted by trust, grudges will turn into forgiveness, discrimination will transform into respect, and hostility into conciliation.

We are no longer living in an era where it is sufficient to feel at peace with our own selves. From now on, each and every individual has to join together in affirming the dignity of life. What

I suggest is to bring the world's people together with a global-scale charter that transcends all differences in people's ethnicity, creed, religion, and way of thinking, and embraces all human hearts.

The peace that we human beings seek is built upon the dignity of our own life, and upon reverence for the lives of others. I urgently hope that now, each of us will grasp the opportunity to shed our feelings of selfishness and greed, and revive our lost spirit of humanitarian love, by joining hands in affirming the immenseness of our innate, sacred nature.

Is this not the best time for us to return to our starting point and create a way of life that will positively affect the lives of the next generation? Shall we not pass along to them a world filled with bright hopes for the future? Whether we do this or not depends on the choices that we make at the present moment.

Here, I would like to invite everyone to join in the Fuji Declaration—an affirmation of the dignity of our own lives and the awe that we feel in face of the lives of others. It was created as an expression of love and respect for the whole of humanity. It offers an opportunity for each of us to become a 'change-maker'—one who rekindles the divine spark in each human heart. In rekindling this divine spark, we can change negative thoughts, words, and actions into positive ones.

Bright, positive words are a creative power that springs from each human being's sublime, sacred consciousness—the consciousness of life itself. It is my belief that by exerting the power of light-filled words in our daily lives, we can unleash the momentum for creating a wondrous future on Earth.

Now is the time when we can make it happen. Starting right now, let us pass along no more negative words to future generations. Let our legacy include no more hostilities, no more wars, no more anger and greed, no more discrimination and conflict, no more poverty and starvation, no more illness. Let our legacy be one of unlimited human potential, dignity, respect, and love.

The decision is up to us.

*May peace prevail on Earth.*

# The Fuji Declaration

## AWAKENING THE DIVINE SPARK
## IN THE SPIRIT OF HUMANITY

### For a civilization of oneness with diversity on planet earth

A new phase in the evolution of human civilization is on the horizon. With deepening states of crisis bringing unrest to all parts of the world, there is a growing need for change in our ways of thinking and acting. We now have the choice of either spiraling into deepening peril, or breaking through to a world of dignity and wellbeing for all.

Throughout its history, humanity has been guided primarily by a material consciousness. Fearing scarcity, we have continued to pursue material gain beyond necessity, taking from others and depleting the Earth's natural resources. If our aspirations continue to focus only on what is material and finite, our world will face inevitable destruction.

## What is our true nature?

In order to make more enlightened choices and change the course of our history, we need to return to the basic question concerning human life. Each and every one of us must ask, "What is our true nature?" and seek a meaningful and responsible answer.

The great spiritual traditions of the world have always been telling us that, at its root, human life is inextricably linked to its universal source. Today, the latest advances in the physical and life sciences reaffirm this perennial insight. When we rediscover our connections to nature and the cosmos, we can re-align our life with the universal movement toward oneness and harmony in and through diversity. We can restore the divine spark in the human spirit and bring forth our innate love, compassion, wisdom, and joy to live a flourishing life. The time has come for every one of us to awaken the divine spark that resides in our heart.

## What is the purpose of our existence?

We have been born at a critical juncture in history, in a world in transition, where it is possible to guide the advancement of humankind toward peace on Earth. Living peace and enabling peace to prevail on Earth is the ultimate purpose for all of us. We can and must embrace it in every sphere of our existence.

By living consciously and responsibly, we can draw upon our inherent freedom and power to shape our destiny and the destiny of humankind. Our task is to collaboratively create a world of dignity and compassion that unfolds the full potential of the human spirit—a world in which every individual gives expression to his or her highest self, in service to the human family and the whole web of life on the planet.

## Toward a new civilization

It is imperative to bring together individuals from diverse fields—scientists, artists, politicians, religious and business leaders, and others—to create a solid multidimensional foundation for catalyzing a timely shift in the course of history. The time has come for all people to become courageous pioneers—to venture beyond their personal, cultural, and national interests and beyond the boundaries of their discipline, and to come together in wisdom, spirit and intention for the benefit of all people in the human family. By so doing, we can overcome the hold of obsolete ideas and outdated behaviors in today's unsustainable world and design a more harmonious and flourishing civilization for the coming generations.

## The paradigm of the new civilization

The paradigm of the new civilization is a culture of oneness with respect for diversity. Just as the myriad cells and diverse organs of our body are interconnected by their oneness and work together in harmony for the purpose of sustaining our life, so each and every living thing is an intrinsic part of the larger symphony of life on this planet. With the conscious recognition that we are all a part of a living universe consisting of great diversity yet embracing unity, we will co-evolve with one another and with nature through a network of constructive and coherent relationships.

## We, as individuals responsible for our and our children's future, hereby declare that:

—We affirm the divine spark in the heart and mind of every human being and intend to live by its light in every sphere of our existence.

—We commit ourselves to fulfilling our shared mission of creating lasting peace on Earth through our ways of living and acting.

—We intend to live and act so as to enhance the quality of life and the well-being of all forms of life on the planet, recognizing that all living things in all their diversity are interconnected and are one.

—We continually and consistently strive to free the human spirit for deep creativity, and to nurture the necessary transformation to forge a new paradigm in all spheres of human activity, including economics, science, medicine, politics, business, education, religion, the arts, communications and the media.

—We shall make it our mission to design, communicate and implement a more spiritual and harmonious civilization—a civilization that enables humankind to realize its inherent potential and advance to the next stage of its material, spiritual, and cultural evolution.

*To sign the declaration, please go to fujideclaration.org*
**Note:** In May 2016, the Soul of WoMen campaign was inaugurated as a project of The Fuji Declaration. For information, kindly visit **fujideclaration.org/soulofwomen**.

# Further Exercises— Nationalities and Cultural Identities

## A

Divine-minded Afghan people
Divine-minded Albanian people
Divine-minded Algerian people
Divine-minded Andorran people
Divine-minded Angolan people
Divine-minded Antiguan and Barbudan people
Divine-minded Argentine people
Divine-minded Armenian people
Divine-minded Australian people
Divine-minded Austrian people
Divine-minded Azerbaijani people

## B

Divine-minded Bahamian people
Divine-minded Bahraini people
Divine-minded Bangladeshi people
Divine-minded Barbadian people
Divine-minded Basotho people (from Lesotho)
Divine-minded Batswana people (from Botswana)
Divine-minded Belarusian people

Divine-minded Belgian people
Divine-minded Belizean people
Divine-minded Beninese people
Divine-minded Bhutanese people
Divine-minded Bolivian people
Divine-minded Bosnian people
Divine-minded Brazilian people
Divine-minded British people
Divine-minded Bruneian people
Divine-minded Bulgarian people
Divine-minded Burkinabe people (from Burkina Faso)
Divine-minded Burmese people
Divine-minded Burundian people

## *C*

Divine-minded Cambodian people
Divine-minded Cameroonian people
Divine-minded Canadian people
Divine-minded Cape Verdean people
Divine-minded Central African people
Divine-minded Chadian people
Divine-minded Chilean people
Divine-minded Chinese people
Divine-minded Colombian people
Divine-minded Comoran people
Divine-minded Congolese people (includes Congo and Democratic
    Republic of the Congo)
Divine-minded Costa Rican people
Divine-minded Croatian people
Divine-minded Cuban people

Divine-minded Cypriot people
Divine-minded Czech people

## *D-E*

Divine-minded Danish people
Divine-minded Djiboutian people
Divine-minded Dominican people (includes Dominica and Dominican
  Republic)
Divine-minded Dutch people
Divine-minded Ecuadorian people
Divine-minded Egyptian people
Divine-minded Emirati people
Divine-minded Equatorial Guinean people
Divine-minded Eritrean people
Divine-minded Estonian people
Divine-minded Ethiopian people

## *F-G*

Divine-minded Fijian people
Divine-minded Finnish people
Divine-minded French people
Divine-minded Gabonese people
Divine-minded Gambian people
Divine-minded Georgian people
Divine-minded German people
Divine-minded Ghanaian people
Divine-minded Greek people
Divine-minded Grenadian people
Divine-minded Guatemalan people
Divine-minded Guinean people (includes Guinea and Guinea-Bissau)

Divine-minded Guyanese people

## *H-I*
Divine-minded Haitian people
Divine-minded Honduran people
Divine-minded Hungarian people
Divine-minded Icelandic people
Divine-minded I-Kiribati people (from Kiribati)
Divine-minded Indian people
Divine-minded Indonesian people
Divine-minded Iranian people
Divine-minded Iraqi people
Divine-minded Irish people (includes Northern Ireland)
Divine-minded Israeli people
Divine-minded Italian people
Divine-minded Ivorian people

## *J-K*
Divine-minded Jamaican people
Divine-minded Japanese people
Divine-minded Jordanian people
Divine-minded Kazakhstani people
Divine-minded Kenyan people
Divine-minded Kittitian and Nevisian people (from Saint Kitts and
　　Nevis)
Divine-minded Kuwaiti people
Divine-minded Kyrgyzstani people

## *L*
Divine-minded Laotian (or Lao) people

Divine-minded Latvian people
Divine-minded Lebanese people
Divine-minded Liberian people
Divine-minded Libyan people
Divine-minded Liechtenstein people
Divine-minded Lithuanian people
Divine-minded Luxembourg people

## *M*

Divine-minded Macedonian people
Divine-minded Malagasi people (from Madagascar)
Divine-minded Malawian people
Divine-minded Malaysian people
Divine-minded Maldivian people
Divine-minded Malian people
Divine-minded Maltese people
Divine-minded Marshallese people
Divine-minded Mauritanian people
Divine-minded Mauritian people
Divine-minded Mexican people
Divine-minded Micronesian people
Divine-minded Moldovan people
Divine-minded Mongolian people
Divine-minded Montenegrin people
Divine-minded Monégasque people (from Monaco)
Divine-minded Moroccan people
Divine-minded Mozambican people

## *N-O*

Divine-minded Namibian people

Divine-minded Nauruan people
Divine-minded Nepali (or Nepalese) people
Divine-minded New Zealand people
Divine-minded Nicaraguan people
Divine-minded Nigerien people (from Niger)
Divine-minded Nigerian people (from Nigeria)
Divine-minded Ni-Vanuatu people (from Vanuatu)
Divine-minded North Korean people
Divine-minded Norwegian people
Divine-minded Omani people

## P-R

Divine-minded Pakistani people
Divine-minded Palauan people
Divine-minded Palestinian people
Divine-minded Panamanian people
Divine-minded Papua New Guinean people
Divine-minded Paraguayan people
Divine-minded Peruvian people
Divine-minded Philippine people
Divine-minded Polish people
Divine-minded Portuguese people
Divine-minded Qatari people
Divine-minded Romanian people
Divine-minded Russian people
Divine-minded Rwandan people

## S

Divine-minded Saint Lucian people
Divine-minded Saint Vincentian people

Divine-minded Salvadoran people
Divine-minded Samoan people
Divine-minded Sammarinese people (from San Marino)
Divine-minded Sao Tomean people
Divine-minded Saudi Arabian people
Divine-minded Senegalese people
Divine-minded Serbian people
Divine-minded Seychellois people
Divine-minded Sierra Leonean people
Divine-minded Singapore people
Divine-minded Slovakian people
Divine-minded Slovenian people
Divine-minded Solomon Islander people
Divine-minded Somali people
Divine-minded South African people
Divine-minded South Korean people
Divine-minded South Sudanese people
Divine-minded Spanish people
Divine-minded Sri Lankan people
Divine-minded Sudanese people
Divine-minded Surinamese people
Divine-minded Swazi people
Divine-minded Swedish people
Divine-minded Swiss people
Divine-minded Syrian people

# *T*

Divine-minded Taiwanese people
Divine-minded Tajik people
Divine-minded Tanzanian people

Divine-minded Thai people
Divine-minded Tibetan people
Divine-minded Timorese people
Divine-minded Togolese people
Divine-minded Tongan people
Divine-minded Trinidadian and Tobagonian people
Divine-minded Tunisian people
Divine-minded Turkish people
Divine-minded Turkmen people
Divine-minded Tuvaluan people

## *U-Z*
Divine-minded Ugandan people
Divine-minded Ukrainian people
Divine-minded United States people
Divine-minded Uruguayan people
Divine-minded Uzbek people
Divine-minded Venezuelan people
Divine-minded Vietnamese people
Divine-minded Yemeni people
Divine-minded Zambian people
Divine-minded Zimbabwean people

**Note:** This list is intended as an example. Please feel free to use the name of any nationality, ethnic or cultural group, or other people not included in this list.

# NOTES

**1:** Unlike contemporary material science, the study of cosmic science is not a process of testing various hypotheses with experiments and observations. Rather, it is pursued by attuning one's mind to divine (absolute) principles.

**2:** In *Genes and Cosmic Essences* by Kazuo Murakami and Masami Saionji, Ms. Saionji comments: *The universe has a will, or law, that is similar to the will of what you [Dr. Murakami] call 'Something Great.' And we are alive because cosmic essences—portions of 'Something Great'— exist within us.* She further explains: *Usually, what we call genes control our physical bodies. But over and above that, there are cosmic essences that contain the will of 'Something Great,' and I define them as being what govern the workings of our genes. . . [Cosmic essences contain] all the will and elements of 'Something Great,' such as love, forgiveness, creativity and freedom.* To read more about cosmic essences, kindly refer to the referenced work.

**3:** This refers to a Symphony of Peace Prayers (SOPP) ceremony held at the United Nations on February 14, 2013, in a special event called United for a Culture of Peace through Interfaith Harmony. For information about the SOPP, visit **www.symphonyofpeaceprayers.com**.

**4:** The phenomenal plane, or phenomenal world, means the tangible world—the world of events, objects, and appearances.

**5:** 'Goi Sensei' refers to Masahisa Goi (1916-1980), the mentor and adoptive father of Masami Saionji. In Japanese, *sensei* means teacher.

**6:** Also mentioned in chapter 1, an SOPP (Symphony of Peace Prayers) is a worldwide, grassroots, multi-religious prayer for peace ceremony that began in Japan in 2005. For more information, visit **www.symphonyofpeaceprayers.com**.

**7:** To find more light-filled words and phrases, see *Think Something Wonderful: Exercises in positive thinking* by Masami Saionji (visit **www.thinksomethingwonderful.net** for more information).

**8:** To learn about handwritten mandalas, please refer to Masami Saionji's book *The Earth Healer's Handbook* or the website **www.earthhealershandbook.net**.

# ABOUT THE AUTHOR

Descended from the Royal Ryuku Family of Okinawa, Masami Saionji was born in Tokyo, Japan. She was educated in Japan at Gakushuin Women's Junior College and studied English in the United States at Michigan State and Stanford Universities. At an early age, she became a Master of Japanese Classical Dance, and taught students for more than ten years.

While in her teens, she came in touch with the peace vision of philosopher Masahisa Goi, who later designated her as his successor and adopted daughter. She now heads several peace organizations, including the Goi Peace Foundation, founded in Japan, and the World Peace Prayer Society, headquartered in New York. She is perhaps best known for her leadership of the international Peace Pole Initiative, which places visual reminders of peace in key locations around the world.

In November 2001, Ms. Saionji was named an honorary member of the Club of Budapest in recognition of her exceptional efforts for world peace. She is the recipient of the Philosopher Saint Shree Dnyaneshwara World Peace Prize (2008), the WON Award honoring distinguished women leaders (2010), and the Dr. Barbara Fields Humanitarian Peace Award (2016).

In February 2013, she had the privilege of presenting the Symphony of Peace Prayers ceremony at the United Nations, in a special event entitled *United for a Culture of Peace through Interfaith Harmony*, which was hosted by the president of the UN General Assembly. In 2015, she initiated the Fuji Declaration along with her husband Hiroo and Dr. Ervin Laszlo.

Masami Saionji has authored over twenty books in Japanese and eleven in English and other languages. She has lived in North America and Europe, and travels extensively on speaking and seminar tours. She and her husband, the descendant of a Japanese prime minister, have three daughters. They currently live in Tokyo.

*The author welcomes your comments, impressions, or experiences concerning this book. Please send them to:*

Masami Saionji – English Publications
Hitoana 812-1
Fujinomiya, Japan 418-0102
E-mail: info@thinksomethingwonderful.net

*Internet users are invited to visit:*

www.goipeace.or.jp
www.worldpeace.org
www.fujideclaration.org
www.thinksomethingwonderful.net
www.earthhealershandbook.net

Printed in Poland
by Amazon Fulfillment
Poland Sp. z o.o., Wrocław

50080315R00111